KNOW WHO YOU ARE,
BE WHAT YOU WANT

David Fontana is a psychologist who holds posts at the University of Wales and the University of Minho, Portugal. For over 25 years he has studied Eastern and Western religions, meditation, dreams, psychotherapy and other techniques for spiritual and psychological development. His many books on psychology and personal growth have been translated into 18 languages.

by the same author

Your Growing Child
Growing Together
The Elements of Meditation
Space in Mind
The Lotus in the City
The Secret Power of Dreams
The Meditator's Handbook

KNOW WHO YOU ARE, BE WHAT YOU WANT

10 STEPS TO SELF-DISCOVERY AND PERSONAL CHANGE

David Fontana

ELEMENT
Shaftesbury, Dorset ● Rockport, Massachusetts ● Brisbane, Australia

Copyright © David Fontana 1992, 1997

First published in 1992 by Fontana,
an imprint of HarperCollins *Publishers*

This edition published in Great Britain in 1997 by
Element Books Limited
Shaftesbury, Dorset SP7 8BP

Published in the USA in 1997 by
Element Books, Inc.
PO Box 830, Rockport, MA 01966

Published in Australia in 1997 by
Element Books Limited
for Jacaranda Wiley Limited
33 Park Road, Milton, Brisbane 4064

Cover design by Mark Slader
Printed and bound in Great Britain by
JW Arrowsmith, Bristol

British Library Cataloguing in Publication
data available

Library of Congress Cataloging in Publication
data available

ISBN 1–85230–884–2

To all those clients with whom
I have worked over the years and
from whom I have learnt so much.

CONTENTS

INTRODUCTION

This book is intended to take you on a journey of self-discovery and of personal change and growth. It contains ten interrelated yet individual steps, the first six designed to help you know who you are, and the remaining four to help you be what you want.

Throughout the book there are exercises to help you on the journey, and case histories to illustrate the circumstances and the progress of others who are on the same path as yourself. Go through the ten steps in the right order. The first six, designed as they are to help you towards self-knowledge, don't tell you how to proceed with your problems once you have identified them. Be patient. The way forward is outlined in the four that follow. But these steps are of limited use unless they build on the first six. As the title of the book indicates, and as the division into two parts emphasizes, you need to know who you are before you can be what you want.

In human psychology, no-one can give you all the right answers. We human beings are much too complex for anything quite so straightforward; we are each of us individuals, with our own ways of being. The purpose of this book is to show you how answers can be found, and to put you in a position to make good use of these answers once you have them. I hope it will prove to be a valuable companion to you on your journey.

PART ONE

KNOW WHO YOU ARE

1

KNOWING YOUR OWN MIND

When we drive a car along the open road we are in charge of what we're doing. We know where we're going, and we know how to get there. We know how to steer round obstacles and corners, how to change gear, how to watch the road in front and behind, how to check our speed and our engine temperature, and how to keep an eye on the level of fuel in our tank. In short, we're responsible for our own decisions and for our own actions.

The same is true of many of the other things we do in life. For example, I'm in charge (if somewhat precariously at times) of the word processor on which I'm typing these words. I can take charge, whenever it suits me, of all the other electrical gadgets around the house. I switch them on when I want to use them, and I switch them off when I've done with them. I'm also in charge of how I handle my bank account and my credit cards, of how quickly I deplete the contents of my wine store, and of the rate at which I add to the books on my bookshelves.

When it comes to the material things with which we choose to surround our daily lives, the things *out there*, we exercise a high level of control. No matter how often we accuse them of having a will of their own, the truth is that the objects and gadgets with which we fill our environment are our servants rather than our masters. The same is true of much of the natural world, which for better or worse we have tamed to our liking. But is it true for the things that go on *inside* our heads as opposed to the things that go on outside them? The things *in here* as opposed to the things out there? In other words, are we in charge of our thoughts and our emotions?

If I were to ask you 'Who's in charge *in here*?' you might

answer '*I* am'. Or, more tentatively, 'Well, I *think* I am'. Or, more tentatively still, 'Well . . . maybe I am, most of the time'. Whichever answer you think you might give, let's start by putting this question to the test:

1. Can you banish thoughts that are worrying or distressing you, whenever you want?

2. Can you replace them with pleasant thoughts (without using drugs of any kind)?

3. Can you stop thinking about *anything at all*, and keep your mind clear whenever you choose and for as long as you choose?

If you can answer yes to all these questions, you hardly need to read any further. But if, like the rest of us, you answer no to them, then you're ready once more for the question 'Who's in charge *in here*?' The following exercise provides a useful starting point in our exploration of this question, an exploration which has many implications for our happiness and the way we live our lives.

▶ **Exercise 1: Watching your thoughts**

Sit comfortably where you can see the hands of a watch or clock. Note the time, then close your eyes. Now stop thinking. Don't keep telling yourself 'I'm not thinking', or 'I mustn't think'. These are still thoughts. Let your mind stay empty. But keep alert. Don't doze or drift into sleep . . . As soon as a thought comes into your mind, open your eyes and look at the time. How long was your mind able to stay clear?

Now close your eyes again and attempt the same exercise. But this time, don't open your eyes when a thought enters your head. Instead, just observe the thought and watch the train of further thoughts set off by it. Follow this train of thought for a few minutes, then when you're tired of it open your eyes.

How long did you stop thinking during the first part of this exercise? More than a minute? A minute? Half a minute? Ten seconds? Five?

The chances are you didn't manage it for more than ten seconds, which is about average for most of us. This probably confirms your answer to question 3 above: you certainly can't stop thinking and keep your mind clear whenever you choose and for as long as you choose. Your thoughts seem to have a power of their own, arising and commanding your attention as they please.

What about the second part of the exercise? Did you notice how one thought seemed to trigger off the next one, which in turn triggered off the next, and so on, in a chain of associations which may have led you from a thought such as 'I wonder why I'm doing this?' to thoughts about the various other things you're asked to do in life . . . to thoughts about what you would do with your life if your time were your own . . . to thoughts about how much you'd like to travel abroad . . . to thoughts about last year's summer holidays . . . to thoughts about next Christmas . . . to thoughts about what you're going to buy for your family as Christmas presents . . . to worries about your bank balance . . . and finally to thoughts about changing your job and earning more money?

No doubt your train of thoughts was quite different. No matter. The important thing is to see how thoughts build up, how one leads to another, and how throughout the process your thoughts seem to have this strange power of their own.

Which raises even more pertinently the question 'Who's in charge *in here*?'

THE POWER OF OUR THOUGHTS

The truth is that usually it isn't the conscious, decision-making part of our mind – the part we tend to think of as our 'self' – that is in charge at all. It isn't that part of our mind that deliberately decides to think about certain issues, or that decides to concentrate, or that decides to relax and stop thinking about anything at all. It is a much deeper part, the 'unconscious' (to use a readily understood term), a part which lies below the surface of our consciousness, and which throws thoughts and ideas and anxieties up into our consciousness much as it pleases, often seeming to take a perverse delight in throwing up the very things it knows will disturb us most, and which we may most want to forget. Thus for example when we are trying to relax, it will suddenly call to mind all the things we 'ought' to be doing. Or when we're trying to concentrate on something important it will keep distracting us with trivia. Or when we're trying to forget a sadness or an embarrassing incident or an unhappy relationship or a mood of depression it will keep reminding us of it.

For most of us, our thoughts are much of the time as out of our control as a brood of unruly children. They dominate us instead of the other way round. They control for much of the time the way we feel and the way in which we experience our lives. Science hasn't yet been clever enough to explain exactly the process of thinking, how ideas are formulated below the level of consciousness and then emerge in the conscious mind as thoughts. But simple observation of your own mind will show you that for much of the time they emerge unbidden. You don't set them off; rather it is they that set off themselves. At times this can be highly beneficial. Creative ideas, inspirational ideas, solutions to problems, happy thoughts enter the mind and are more than welcome. But this book is about those thoughts that have a negative effect upon us, that intrude between us and happiness, that influence our moods, our picture of ourselves, our wellbeing in ways that we would much rather be without.

It is important that we reach a better understanding of these thoughts, and find ways of changing and controlling them so that they no longer lead to the unhappiness that we may have been feeling. Negative thoughts about ourselves for example, about our abilities, about our value as individuals, together with mistaken or inaccurate ideas about other people, about our relationships with them, and about how they see us, lead us to much unnecessary anxiety and hinder us from growing and developing psychologically in the ways we want. It is indeed possible to reach this understanding, but in order to do so we must first take two vital steps:

Step 1: acknowledge the extent of the hold our thoughts have over us; the mistaken idea that it is really we who are in charge won't do – the problem can't be tackled unless we admit its existence in the first place.

Step 2: find out more about what it is in our life experience that has prompted us to have the kind of thoughts we have, so that we can start to bring about the changes to them that will help us live a more fulfilled and contented life.

Exercise 1 has helped us with the first step, and modern practical psychology can do much to help us with the second.

Modern practical psychology is concerned with all aspects of human thinking and behaviour, but the area that interests us in this case is the extensive body of knowledge built up over the years on how to recognize and deal with the problems that give rise to anxiety, depression, panic, frustration, rage, guilt, jealousy and the other unhappy states that afflict our inner lives. Modern practical psychology doesn't have all the answers, but for those who are prepared to listen to what it has to say and put a little time and energy into its techniques it can go a long way towards bringing about a fundamental and permanent change in the quality of our lives, since it helps us to study ourselves, to get to know who we really are and what we really want, and to take the course of our future development more into our own hands.

But before we go into the relevant areas of psychology more deeply, we have some more preliminary self-examination to do.

THE POWER OF OUR EMOTIONS

Our thoughts represent only part of our inner life. The other part is made up of our emotions and our feelings. This part can have just as much effect on our sense of wellbeing. It is our emotions that give life its texture, its colour, its impact upon us. A life composed only of thinking would be a singularly dull and arid one. Positive emotions such as joy, excitement, interest and love are what make our lives feel happy, while negative emotions such as sadness, fear and anger are what make it feel unhappy. If we are to work on ourselves to improve the quality of our psychological lives, then we must get to know more about our emotions – where they come from and how to handle them – as well as get to know more about our thoughts.

Emotions and thoughts are inextricably linked. When we feel our spirits rise, our thoughts are likely to follow. When our thoughts are pleasant ones, our spirits rise in turn, and the opposite is equally true. We've all had the experience of troubled thoughts prompting troubled emotions – which prompt further troubled thoughts which lead to further troubled emotions and so on, spiralling downwards. Thoughts and emotions are so influenced by each other that in working to improve our psychological wellbeing, we should think of them as partners.

In the light of this close link between the two parts of our inner life, it isn't really surprising that when we ask 'Who's in charge *in here?*' about our emotions, we're likely to get essentially the same answer that we did when enquiring about our thinking. Test this by asking yourself the original three questions, rephrased this time to apply to emotions:

1. Can you terminate a negative emotion that is worrying or distressing you, whenever you want?

2. Can you replace it with a positive emotion (without using drugs of any kind)?

3. Can you prevent unwanted emotions arising, and

keep your feelings clear and calm whenever you
choose and for as long as you choose?

If you answered 'no' to any or all of these questions you're
in good company. Most people give the same answer. And
what this answer tells us is that we're no more in charge of
our emotions than we are of our thoughts.

We can now go back to Steps 1 and 2, and enlarge them
to apply to emotions as well as to thoughts. They now read
like this:

Step 1: we must acknowledge the extent of the hold of
both thoughts and emotions over us; the self-delusion
that it is really we who are in charge won't do – a
problem can't be tackled unless we admit its existence
in the first place.

Step 2: we must find out more about our own thought
and emotional processes and ways of handling them,
so that we can bring them more under the control of
our conscious mind.

The more we ponder how little control we really have over
our thoughts and our emotions, the more we recognize the
need to ask ourselves how this lack of control came about.
In order to answer this question, we must take a short trip
back into our childhood, into the formative years when so
many of the foundations of the people we now are were
being laid. This is the first of several such trips we're going
to make.

A CHILD'S-EYE VIEW OF THE WORLD

When we're children, we're taught all kinds of essential
lessons on how to handle the world. We're taught through
the use of language and maths and science how to interact
with the environment around us, how to solve problems,
how to take part in activities, how to understand links
between physical causes and physical effects. We're taught

how, in short, to be in charge *out there*. But we get precious little help on how to be in charge *in here*, how to understand our mental and emotional lives. Small wonder then that so many of us spend a large part of our lives caught up in thoughts we'd rather not be thinking, or in the grip of emotions we'd rather not be feeling. Small wonder that much of the time we feel powerless to change the aspects of our mental or emotional lives that we want to change (such as over-anxiety, unnecessary feelings of anger and irritation, low self-esteem, depressed moods, guilt, or an inability to assert ourselves when necessary), or to live our lives in the joyful and enriching way that we would like.

It's Not Your Fault

Working with people who are unhappy about their lives, I usually find they have a deep-seated belief that the things that have gone wrong are essentially their own fault (see box). They talk about their inadequacies, their weaknesses, their disgust or anger with themselves. They refer to 'my problem' as if it's a sign of their own failure as a human being, as if it's their own creation, sustained by personality flaws for which they alone are responsible. They say things like 'I know it's my own fault', 'I'm so stupid', 'I've only myself to blame', 'I get so mad with myself about it'. They show themselves heroically unaware of the true history of their problems, and of the part this history plays in preventing them from dealing with these problems and freeing themselves from the legacy of the past.

BLAME AND GUILT

Since self-blame – and the guilt that goes with it – figures so largely in the lives of many of us, and is responsible for so many of our negative feelings about ourselves and our lives, something more needs to be said about it.

As I have indicated, we shouldn't blame ourselves for our inability to handle many of the psychological difficulties

---

that we experience. If we think objectively, we can see that most of us received little help in learning how to deal with these difficulties; in learning, in other words, how to deal with what goes on *in here*. So why this readiness to blame ourselves for them? And why the guilt that goes with this blame?

The answer is that in our early development we always experienced blame as a one-way process. Long before we were old enough to see that the adults in our lives were fallible creatures who got things wrong sometimes, we had plentiful experience of being told of our own errors. Thus getting things wrong became always what *I* do, not what other people do.

By the time we were old enough to apportion blame more accurately, we had it deeply ingrained in our mind that 'blame' was essentially something that belonged to 'me'. The guilt that goes with blame is essentially the self-punishment that we internalize and inflict upon ourself in addition to the punishment inflicted upon us by others. We carry this deeply ingrained attitude into adult life. If we're being punished for something, we feel – in spite of evidence to the contrary – that somehow we must be at fault.

So painful are the feelings associated with 'blame' and 'guilt' that when we eventually learn as a child that other people can be 'blamed' too, we may try to avoid suffering these feelings by attempting always to shift responsibility on to someone else. 'It's not *my* fault' becomes an insistent cry.

This is of course just as unrealistic as feeling one is to blame for everything. What we should have learned is how to be balanced and objective about apportioning responsibility for the things that go wrong, ready to accept our share of the blame or to allocate it elsewhere as appropriate.

The other thing we should learn is that when the blame really is ours, analysing why a situation went wrong and learning from it is much more use to us than carrying a burden of guilt. To forgive others is healthy, and it is equally healthy to forgive ourselves as well – provided our regret for avoidable mistakes is genuine and we have done all we can to atone for any harm we may have caused. Knowing how properly to apologize to others helps this process of forgiveness, just as knowing how to accept their apologies helps them in their turn.

To the two vital steps listed on page 11 we must now add a third:

Step 3: we must recognize that given the little help most of us have received on how to be in charge of our inner lives, there's no point blaming ourselves if we're not yet very good at it.

However, the fact that we're given so little help in understanding and shaping our inner lives during our early formative years doesn't mean we should shift the blame for our present problems on to the parents and teachers who failed to give us the guidance we needed. They probably didn't receive much guidance either, so naturally hadn't much to offer. Most of the human race is left to struggle alone with what goes on *in here.* Even the most loving and sympathetic parent or partner or friend – though their love and their sympathy can be a great support in itself – is not equipped by their own background to know how to guide us through our inner difficulties or to know how to teach us to guide ourselves.

THE PRESSURES OF MODERN LIFE

In addition to the lack of guidance we received from others, our problems *in here* are made worse by the sheer complexity of our highly industrialized and highly artificial way of life. Compare your own life experience to date with that of someone living as recently as fifty or a hundred years ago. Economic hardship may be much less of a problem now, but throughout your life you have been faced with a far greater range of influences, many of them in conflict with each other, than were your grandparents or even your parents.

The expectations people have of themselves and of each other change in the modern world at a bewildering speed. Values and patterns of behaviour alter in style and in meaning almost over months, when once they changed only over the centuries: the 'successful' man or woman is a very different creature nowadays from what he or she was in the early decades of the twentieth century. And now the dangers and threats from the environment, which once came in the form of localized poverty and disease, arrive in the form of potential global catastrophe. Life nowadays puts far greater pressure on our ability to cope psychologically than it did when our grandparents were young.

This pressure is compounded by the fact that as our civilization 'develops', our environment becomes ever more artificial and cut off from the natural world. This means that in childhood and adolescence we live in a world hedged in by man-made taboos. Life in a modern home, for instance, with new carpets on the floor, expensive electrical gadgets in every room, breakable objects on every surface, a shiny new car in the garage and potentially lethal power tools in the shed, means that the embargoes placed upon children not to make a mess, not to touch, not to meddle, not to explore become ever more insistent. The environment becomes a place of restrictions, a place of dos and don'ts far more pressing (and even less understandable to a child's mind) than the taboos of earlier generations.

This distancing from the natural world, the world in which we evolved and with which nature has given us a relationship, also means that a child misses the stimulation and the comfort of daily communion with open spaces, with the sights, sounds and colours of the countryside, with the experience of long rambling walks, with the need to use his or her eyes and ears, with the feel of rain and wind and of the freedom and expanding horizons which close encounters with nature bring to the self image and the human spirit. I live near a primary school. Many of the children who attend it pass my study window twice a day. The great majority are whisked past in the backs of cars, usually slumped down almost out of sight. Few families in this area live farther than a ten-minute walk from the school. Yet each day children are denied the opportunity, when starting and ending the school day, to take a close look at the world in which they live.

Placing children in a very different environment from the one in which, over thousands of years, human evolution has taken place influences profoundly the way they experience and understand their lives, and the way in which they think of themselves. Inevitably an 'unnatural' life surrounds them with frustrations and confusions, and makes understanding and coming to terms with what is going on *in here* ever more difficult.

Just as bewildering for children are the conflicting messages they receive from the people around them. As a child you were taught a basic moral code, a basic pattern of behaviour, at school and by your parents; yet nightly on television, or in the books you read, you found people living by completely different standards, and often appearing to find success and happiness as a result. In so many areas of life you were faced with the fact that the principles and assumptions teachers and parents taught you were being contradicted everywhere you looked.

Things don't suddenly and miraculously become easier when you're an adult. Modern living has freed us from much of the drudgery of the past, and even from many of the injustices. But adults in the modern Western world have their own crosses to bear.

In a modern industrialized and computerized society, carefully acquired skills and qualifications can become abruptly outdated and unwanted. Redundancies can come out of the blue. Jobs can disappear overnight. Familiar landmarks in the environment can vanish without trace. The securities by which we orientate our lives and which help give us our identity can be whisked away from us. Marriages and relationships can break up, families fall apart, neighbours and friends be lured away by better prospects on the other side of the country or the other side of the world, financial crises arrive unheralded, and new physical hazards like AIDS or poisoned food or polluted air and water or global warming force themselves on our consciousness.

For many people – especially women – there are also conflicts between career and family, between taking a desirable job outside the home and giving the children the attention they need and deserve. And always there is the pressure of time. Modern living never seems to allow enough time in twenty-four hours to get everything done, let alone to relax and give some proper thought to what goes on *in here*. Instead, *in here* all too often becomes a set of guilty thoughts about divided loyalties and all the things half done or left undone, a set of nagging thoughts and their attendant emotions about our own inadequacy, which rub in yet more deeply the fact that, wherever else we may be in charge, we certainly aren't in charge *in here*.

Finally, with the decline in conventional religious beliefs and values, the modern world can often seem stripped of its meaning. What, in the end, is all the struggling and striving, the running hard just to stay in the same place, actually *for*? Why do we do it? Even the extra income, the material goods, the holidays abroad, can fail to satisfy. Somewhere, somehow, between this and that, between all the frantic comings and goings, the fragile magical concept of meaning has slipped away.

NO WONDER WE HAVE PROBLEMS!

If from childhood onwards we not only receive little direct help with what goes on *in here*, but face circumstances *out there* which make dealing with life quite difficult in the first place, it is small wonder that so many of us experience anxiety, fear, depression and all the other states that make life uncomfortable. The daunting truth is that at some time in our lives one in ten of us (one in eight women and one in twelve men – we'll look at the possible reasons for the statistical imbalance between the sexes in Chapter 3) will seek psychiatric help for these problems. And many more of us will rely on our doctors for tranquillizers or sleeping pills, or come to *depend* on socially acceptable drugs like alcohol or caffeine or nicotine to help us get through our days and our nights, thus losing even more direct control over our own minds.

Taking the circumstances of modern living into account, it would be surprising if we didn't have these problems, at least in some areas of our lives, which brings us to the fourth step towards a greater understanding of *in here*. We must:

Step 4: recognize that the possession of psychological problems isn't a sign of weakness.

However – and this is crucial – *it may well become a sign of weakness if we don't attempt to do something about our psychological problems*. There's no law that says they have simply to be endured. There's no law that says only someone *out there* can do something about them for us. There's no law that says we're helpless to do anything about them for ourselves. Our helplessness is caused more by lack of knowledge than by lack of ability.

Doing something about our own problems may not seem an easy option. But then, mastering any worthwhile set of skills – and learning to use psychology in our lives is essentially about learning a set of skills – is never easy. It demands a little time and effort, and the patience and courage to work through setbacks instead of being thrown by them. It demands some knowledge of theory, and the determination to put theory into practice.

Mastering the use of psychology in our lives is no less worthy of our time and effort than mastering other skills. Quite the contrary. It is unquestionably among the most important learning experiences of our lives, since it can help us become the whole and effective people nature intended us to be. The only wonder is that although we happily spend much time and money mastering other learning tasks, we are often so reluctant to give attention to this one. And we subject ourselves to much unnecessary mental and emotional suffering as a consequence.

Learning how to understand our own psychology in order to help us live happier and more stress-free lives may seem difficult at first because we have already acquired many bad psychological habits and techniques which can hinder our progress, and which may need to be unlearnt. It's rather like taking up what we think is a new interest or hobby, only to find that we've been practising it already every day of our lives, but in the wrong way and in the wrong frame of mind.

However, learning to understand our own psychology has a major advantage over other kinds of learning: it is that we carry our inner lives, what I am calling *in here*, around with us all the time. We don't have to get up from a comfortable armchair in the evening and go to another room (or go out to an evening class) in order to start understanding and working on ourselves. We don't have to get out any apparatus or materials. We don't have to spend any money. We don't have to pass any tests (except the ones we set ourselves). We don't have to drop any of our other interests, absent ourselves from family and friends, travel to another part of the country, change jobs. *In here* is going on all the time. Working on it simply means applying new ways of thinking about it, new ways of understanding, new ways of looking at and using our feelings. And we don't have to wait until next week or next month for the term to start. We can begin here, this very moment.

2

YOU HAVE THE POWER
TO CHANGE

There is a very great deal we can do in order to become more in charge of what happens *in here*. We can go a long way towards understanding ourselves better, towards understanding the origins of our psychological problems and what sustains them, and towards developing ways of handling them. We can now formulate this as Step 5:

> *Step 5:* acknowledge that you have the power to change things – it is possible for you to be more fully in charge of your inner life.

If we are to begin the process of taking charge, we need first to look at the relationship between what goes on *in here* and what goes on *out there*. I said in Chapter 1 that from childhood onwards we are taught a great deal about the material things in our environment *out there*, and this is true. But some of the lessons we're taught are highly misleading, and provide us with further difficulties in getting to know more about *in here*.

SOME MISLEADING LESSONS ABOUT
OUT THERE

The lessons are concerned with the information we are given that the world and the things that happen in it *out there* are hard material facts. Facts that exist, solid and definite, beyond doubt and argument. But is this information true? With the collaboration of another member of the family or of a friend, put it to the test:

▶ Exercise 2: Describing objects

Go with your collaborator to a window and look out at a familiar scene. The street, your garden or whatever it happens to be. Look at it together for an agreed length of time – say a minute – and then without consulting each other, and without going to the window again, both write down what you saw. Make the two sets of descriptions as detailed as you can, and take as long over them as each of you wishes. When you've both finished, have a look at the descriptions.

What do you notice about them? Are they the same? Even when the same objects are described, is the language used to describe them identical? Are the objects named by each of you mentioned in the same order? Do you both make reference to the same colours? To the same shapes? To the same impressions? Are both descriptions the same length? Are both equally interesting?

As you look at the two sets of descriptions you'll see that, although they both refer to one and the same scene, they differ significantly from each other. What does this tell us? You were both looking at the same things. Why aren't the two sets of descriptions identical?

'Well,' you may say, 'we're two different people; the descriptions are bound to be different.' Precisely. We take this kind of thing for granted. But think about it for a moment. If what is *out there* is the same for you both in terms of hard facts, then surely your descriptions should be the same? The whole point of this exercise is to remind you that it *isn't* the same. We each view the world selectively. We take most notice of the things that are important to us. One person may pay more attention to the trees, flowers and growing things. Another to the houses and cars. Another to the people passing by. Another to the cat sitting on the wall or the dog nosing around the lawn.

One person may note the colour of each of the objects he or she is describing (a red car passing by, a woman in a brown coat waiting for the bus, a dark grey cloud overhead). Another may ignore colour altogether and make several references to size (a small willow tree, a large coach full of tourists, a diminutive grey squirrel half-hidden in the branches). Another person may leave out certain details altogether, as if he or she hasn't seen them, while another may exaggerate trivial details and another give a rather dull list of nouns.

If you were asked to say how you *felt* about the things you were describing, the differences would be even more marked. One person would enjoy the view from the window, another would find it depressing. One person would find it interesting and full of incident, another would find it dull. We all of us project our feelings, the way we are experiencing ourselves *in here*, on to the world that presents itself to us *out there*.

For further examples of the selective way in which we experience the world, look at the way two painters, using the same techniques, paint similar scenes. Or at the way two novelists describe their characters and the things that happen to them. Or at the way two poets use words. Or at the way two newspapers present the news.

▶ Exercise 3: Describing events

Try your own variation of this experiment. Again with the help of another person, and following the same practice of writing down your descriptions independently and each in your own time, give a written account of a simple event in which you were both recently involved. Afterwards compare the accounts.

Again you'll see the same kind of differences emerge. So much so in fact that you may wonder whether you're both writing about the same thing. This 'unreliability' of eye-witness accounts, no matter how sincere the witnesses, is the bane of lawyers and police officers (and

of teachers and parents!) when attempting to obtain details
of key incidents.

▶ Exercise 4: Describing other people

Now try another experiment. Again with the help of
someone else, and again working independently, write
down descriptions of a person well known to you both.
Include all you can about his or her appearance,
personality, interests, strengths, weaknesses and the
like. Try and give the kind of description that would be
useful to a third party who has never met the person
you're both writing about. When the exercise is over,
compare notes.

What do you discover? Predictably, once again there are
marked discrepancies between the two accounts. If you
discuss them together, you'll find yourselves saying to
each other such things as, 'Oh I don't see him/her like
that at all'. 'No, I disagree; I think he/she is much
nicer/prettier/kinder/more reliable/more trustworthy than
you do,' and so on.

OUR SUBJECTIVE WORLD

What we learn from these exercises is that, far from being
solid and definite, what happens *out there* is very much a
matter of personal interpretation. We each live in our own
subjective world. What happens *out there* is filtered through
what is happening *in here*. We make sense of the world
each in our own way. The things, the events, the people
out there are reconstructed for us by our own thoughts and
our own emotions. A simple little story illustrates this very
well. Two people, one a pessimist and one an optimist, are
looking at a bottle of wine from which half has already been
drunk. 'Oh dear,' says the pessimist gloomily, 'the bottle is
already half empty.' 'Oh good,' says the optimist, 'the bottle
is still half full.'

The difference between the two ways of looking at the bottle and what it represents is crucial. The pessimist interprets life by noticing and stressing the negative things, the optimist by noticing and stressing the positive. Which of them is right?

Is the bottle half empty or half full? It's for you to say. But think of this: when the pessimist draws back the bedroom curtains in the morning and looks out at the world, and notices the clouds and says it's going to be a rotten day, for him or her it will be. And when the optimist draws back the curtains and notices the beautiful patterns the clouds make and that it isn't raining, and decides it's going to be a good day, for him or her it will be.

This doesn't mean that trying our hardest to be optimistic about anything and everything will put the world to rights. Some optimists remain so determinedly cheerful that they overlook genuine difficulties and take no action to correct them until it's too late. Optimism and pessimism are two extreme ways of looking at the world; we all of us find our place somewhere between them.

But we aren't stuck with our current outlook. There are ways of changing it, as we shall see.

How Do I See Me?

There's one more experiment we need to try before the theme of this chapter is fully clear. This is a more demanding one, and if you feel a little threatened by it, simply imagine yourself going through it and exploring the outcome. You don't have to attempt it with someone else unless you feel ready to do so.

▶ Exercise 5: Describing yourself

A friend or a member of the family is needed if you want to do the exercise in full. It must be someone who knows you well, likes you, and can be relied upon to be open and straightforward about you. Again work independently, each in your own time. Again each of you must write a description, but this time the descriptions you both write are about *you*. In your own description, write about yourself in the *third* person rather than the first, 'David is . . .' rather than 'I am . . .'

As when writing about someone else in Exercise 4, you and the person working with you must each attempt as full a picture of you as possible. You must both give a physical description of you, give your likes and dislikes, your strengths and weaknesses, your personality, your interests and hobbies, your attitudes towards this and that, and so on. Above all, both of you must be as honest and objective as possible about you, without, of course, trying to be deliberately unkind.

When the exercise is over, compare notes. Look for similarities and differences. Look for surprises. Does the other person have the same kind of picture of you as you have of yourself? Does he or she see you in a more or in a less favourable light? Does he or she know about your interests, your attitudes, your temperament, the things that are important or unimportant to you? As with the results of Exercises 2, 3 and 4, neither you nor the other person is 'right' in the sense that your picture is a totally accurate one. Both you and he or she are filtering the descriptions of you through the ideas, thoughts and feelings each of you has about you.

The important thing to notice is that the picture you have of yourself, of the person you think you are, involves the same kind of subjectivity as the picture you have of the world outside your window. It is, in an important sense, your own creation, just as your descriptions of the view from the window or of another person are. And like them, it can be changed as you come to know and understand yourself better, and come to acknowledge the power you have over your own life.

To revert to the example of the optimist and the pessimist, you can picture yourself in either a positive or a negative light. And if you're unhappy with the way the picture looks, you can begin to consider changing it, just as the half empty bottle can be changed into a half full one.

The exercises we have carried out so far in this chapter make it clear that although we are in charge of much of what happens *out there*, this doesn't mean our picture of *out there* is an objective one. Our knowledge of it is filtered through what is happening *in here*, and our interpretations of it are very much the product of our own individuality – which means essentially of our own thoughts and emotions. Once we realize this, it's easier to recognize that these interpretations can be changed.

It's also easier to recognize the interdependence of *out there* and *in here*. At every moment of our lives each influences the other, to such an extent, in fact, that although the focus of this book is upon our inner experience – as it is this inner experience that represents who we really are – we must never lose sight of this interdependence. Since the way in which we view the world *out there* is influenced by what goes on *in here*, it follows that by changing the latter we can also in an important sense change the former.

For example, it's a simple fact of life that I can't stop it raining today. I can't stop the years passing. I can't stop a bad-tempered motorist hooting at me because he or she dislikes the way I'm driving. I can't stop politicians the world over from behaving like politicians. Maybe I can't even stop a difficult colleague at work from behaving badly towards everyone, or stop a passer-by from playing a radio too loudly, or stop the prices from going up in the shops. But I can do something about the way in which I interpret and react to these things, just as I can change my interpretation of the half-empty/half-full wine bottle. By so doing, I can change the effect they have upon me.

One way of illustrating this is to write down some of the individuals and things in your environment which you dislike, and say what effect these irritations have on you.

▶ **Exercise 6: Things you dislike**

Make a list of some of the people or events or things to which you take objection. Against each one, write down the effect he/she/it has upon you.

Now let's look at the results. If you're like most people, your list will contain the names of three or four people (colleagues, neighbours, public figures, members of the family) and rather more events and things (injustices of some sort, an ugly building that blocks out the view, a car that refuses to start, trains running late, delays at airports, examinations, the dentist, poor service in shops and restaurants, wretched holiday weather, traffic jams, aggressive behaviour and so on).

Against each of the items on your list you will have written things like 'makes me angry', 'frightens me', 'upsets me', 'threatens me', 'makes me feel insecure', 'makes me feel inadequate', 'confuses me', 'makes me sad', 'makes me feel guilty'.

Now locate the magic buttons (on your chest maybe, your forehead, in the pit of your stomach?) that the people and events on your list come and press in order to 'make' you upset, sad, frightened, angry or whatever.

Can you find them? No? Then are we really correct in saying that it's these people and events that are responsible for our bad feelings? Can another person or an event or an object actually 'make' these feelings arise? *Make* these feelings arise? If so, how do they do it? If there are no magic buttons, perhaps you can find some puppet strings they come up and pull? Or a computer drive that they feed with programmed commands? No? So who or what is it that 'makes' us feel as we do? The answer is: it can only be ourselves.

If this seems hard to accept, ask yourself whether you always react in the same way to the irritations out there in your life? Are you *always* nervous that a ring on the telephone is going to bring bad news? Are you *always* impatient at the mistakes or the demands of your colleagues? Are you *always* irritated at the slow-moving motorist in front? If you are a parent, do you *always* snap at your children for just being children? Do you *always* wake low-spirited in the mornings? Do you *always* feel embarrassed in company? Do you *always* hate yourself for making a simple mistake?

There's a good chance the answer is no to most of these questions. Psychological research shows that we fluctuate a great deal in our responses to things *out there*. We have a word for this – 'mood'. It's a word most of us are quite happy to use about others, but less ready to use about ourselves. We have a tendency to put our own fluctuations in behaviour down to circumstances, for example the crassness of those around us, the fact that we're in a hurry, the fact that this or that piece of equipment is always breaking down, the fact that everyone is ganging up on us or that we're so badly misunderstood by those who should know better.

But there's no avoiding the issue. If the world outside influences the way I feel, then in the absence of magic buttons, puppet strings or computer input slots, I have to recognize that ultimately I must take some responsibility for this. Obviously I would be a very strange person if I didn't react to the outside events that happen to me. But unless I realize the part I myself play in this reaction, then I've little chance of gaining more control over what happens *in here*.

People usually respond to this realization in one of two ways. Either they object with 'Yes, but I can't help the way I feel. I don't press any buttons either; the feelings just come up of their own accord, there's nothing I can do about them,' or they argue that even though the emotions concerned may be unpleasant at the time, the fact that we do respond with things like anger and fear to outside events is often a good thing. Anger and fear and the other so-called negative emotions give us the motivation to do something about the outside world, instead of sitting back and accepting whatever it chooses to throw at us.

Both these objections are partly true. And although the first one only re-emphasizes the fact we're not yet in charge of what goes on *in here*, the second says something new. It reminds us of a belief that many people have, which is that psychologists aim to help people cope with their problems by stopping them from thinking and feeling spontaneously, turning them instead into calculating machines who have everything so tightly under control that they cease to bear much relation to flesh-and-blood human beings.

Few beliefs could be farther from the truth. The psychology we're talking about doesn't involve rigid control of the inner life. It involves an understanding of what is taking place in the inner life, an understanding of why we feel and think and behave as we do, and an understanding of how best to tackle those aspects of ourselves which cause us unnecessary suffering and distress. Emotions like anger and fear obviously have a very useful role to play. Mother nature (or evolution) would not have put them there if this were not the case. But there is a big difference between this useful, self-constructive role and the useless, self-destructive one that we so often allow them to assume.

The way to distinguish between these two roles is to establish whether or not the emotion, when it arises, leads to desirable change of some kind. Anger may help us, for example, to right a wrong, to release harmful frustrations, to let others know exactly how we feel and thus allow us to claim our rights and others to understand us better. Or it may make matters worse, needlessly harming or upsetting others, leaving us fretting and fuming and annoyed or ashamed with ourselves when we've had time to calm down.

Good psychology is concerned with giving us more power over our lives, not with robbing us of the things that make us effective and spontaneous human beings. It's concerned with helping us make better use of our humanity rather than less. It's concerned with helping us feel more at home in our lives, to be truer to ourselves and to our real feelings, more at ease socially, more understanding of ourself and of others. It doesn't aim to make us deny or over-control our thoughts and emotions. It aims to free us from being over-controlled *by them*, so that we can begin to shape our lives more as we would wish, and become happier and better-balanced people. In short, so that we can become better able to participate in life and help others do the same, and better equipped to find meaning and purpose in the strange, difficult, exasperating, magical experience of human existence.

WHEN IS A PROBLEM A PROBLEM?

Put at its simplest, a psychological problem is any state of mind which interferes with our sense of psychological wellbeing, just as a physical problem is any state of blood, flesh or bone which interferes with our sense of bodily wellbeing. Put like this, all the things that upset us could come under the heading of psychological problems; most of us are brimful of such upsets from time to time. Happily, though, most of these psychological upsets, like most physical upsets, are short-lived. You have an argument with a colleague or a member of the family, and for a while afterwards you feel hurt about it, but then, just like a bruise on your arm, the hurt quickly fades.

The psychological problems really worthy of the name are those upsets that refuse to fade, or that happen all too easily and all too frequently. If I'm hurt or upset or irritated or prone to fly into a rage whenever anyone says anything out of place to me, then there's an underlying psychological issue that needs attention, just as if I bruise every time I merely brush against something there may be a medical one that needs investigating.

Getting to Know Your Problem

Giving this attention to the psychological issues that have become problems for us doesn't mean constantly returning to and dwelling upon them in the way that our tongue keeps probing an aching tooth. It means, in ways that will be discussed as we go through this book, coming to understand their true nature and their origins, and employing strategies to lay them to rest. And by understanding the true nature of an issue I don't mean merely labelling it. Labels, and the descriptions that go with them, are useful as a start, but we have to go beyond them and identify the specific way in which they apply to us, and the specific meaning they have for our individual lives.

For example, again in ways that will be discussed as we go through the book, *anxiety* is the label for the most common psychological problem, indeed for the problem that in one form or another underlies nearly all the problems we will be talking about. We can describe anxiety as typically involving feelings of apprehension, of insecurity, of uncertainty, and at times of dread and foreboding. When we're anxious we feel in a state of psychological tension, with unhappy thoughts intruding into and dominating our minds in the way I've already described. We commonly experience physical symptoms like a dry mouth, clammy palms, nervous headaches, and shaky limbs, and we may find it hard to concentrate and to remember things. Since anxiety uses up a lot of nervous energy we may feel worn out much of the time, and may even make ourselves physically ill, as the body's resistance to many ailments, from the common cold to backaches and skin disorders, may decrease at such a time.

Helpful as this description is, it doesn't take us very far along the road to understanding and dealing with *our* particular anxiety. We need to go further and say, for instance, that in our case anxiety is a problem, not because it is aroused by the occasional big issue that would trouble most people (a serious illness in the family, a mortgage we suddenly find we can't pay, a broken relationship), but because it seems to be touched off by minor things that others seem to take in their stride (the odd hard word from the boss, the prospect of public-speaking, ordinary decisions about ordinary daily events). Or because even when we've nothing specific to worry about we have vague feelings that things are too good to last (psychologists call this 'free-floating anxiety' – anxiety that is simply waiting for something to attach itself to).

Even this doesn't take us far enough. We need to go

deeper still and start to take a long close look at our anxiety, to start to know it better, and to identify its extent and the things with which it is most often associated.

PHILIP: ANXIOUS ONLY SOME OF THE TIME

A case study will help to illustrate this. Philip was a 25-year-old university graduate who described himself as 'a very anxious person – in a perpetual state of near bloody panic'. He worried, he said, about virtually everything, from his relationship with his girlfriend to his job to the state of his health to the odd noises he fancied his car was always making.

Philip was asked to keep a written record of his state of mind for an average week, scoring himself on the hour every hour during the waking day on a five-point scale from 1 (no anxiety) to 5 (maximum anxiety). He found to his great surprise that scores of 1 and 2 outnumbered scores of 4 and 5. He also found that instead of 'worrying about virtually everything' his worries tended to be specific to areas of his life where he was unsure of his own worth or his abilities. On the strength of this, Philip was forced to agree that it would be more accurate to describe himself as 'a very anxious sort of person *some* of the time and about *some* of the things in my life'.

The truth of the matter was that Philip was free of anxiety more often than not. But the fact that he had got into the habit of thinking of himself as highly anxious about everything meant that he was forever drawing his attention to his anxious moments. Each of these moments was a confirmation to him of his anxious personality, while the moments when he was free of anxiety passed unnoticed, dismissed unconsciously as irrelevant to his image of himself. Philip's was a classic case of *selective attention*. Because he thought of himself as an anxious person, only anxious moments were allowed to score on his internal personality record. He became acutely self-aware whenever he felt anxious, and much less self-aware when he felt good.

Once Philip recognized this fact, part of the solution to his problem was to become more self-aware during the good times, and thus to put the anxious moments more into perspective. To begin with he did this by maintaining his written self-ratings on the hour every hour, but soon he found this was no longer necessary. His mind was automatically picking up on the good times instead of just the bad. And when he was in an anxious mood, he reported that he was no longer so 'anxious about being anxious'. He knew now that the anxiety would pass, and that he wasn't doomed to live as a 'very anxious personality' throughout his life.

It is often a conviction that 'I can't escape from my anxiety or depression or guilt or whatever it is that's troubling me now, and I never will be able to escape from it' that makes life so difficult for many of those with psychological problems. Helping them to see that there are some good moments (or at the very least some moments when things are less black), and that their lives are not entirely dominated by their problems, is a necessary first step in getting them to discard this way of thinking.

▶ **Exercise 7: Recording your state of mind**

The exercise given to Philip is a most effective way of improving self-knowledge. It needs to be done consistently, though. It's of limited value to score yourself only when you think about it. There's a real risk that you'll only think about it at bad times. It's helpful to have a watch that bleeps on the hour. Prepare a pocket notebook with the date at the top of the page and the hours marked off down the left-hand side, and simply write down a score from 1 to 5 each time the watch tells you it's time to do so.

You can try the exercise with whatever state of mind you want to explore, whether it's anxiety, as in Philip's case, or fear, anger, depression or whatever. If you're wanting to get an accurate picture of all your states of mind, jot down an initial for whatever state you're in every time the watch bleeps: 'R' for relaxed, 'E' for excited, 'H' for happy, 'G' for guilty and so on, and where possible make a note of what has prompted it.

This gives you a profile for each day, and after a week or so this builds into a very revealing picture.

When trying this exercise, some people find they're puzzled to know exactly *how* they feel each time they have to keep their record. The watch bleeps, and they find themselves asking 'Mmm yes, but how *do* I feel?'. For them, the answer isn't an obvious one. If this applies to you, don't be discouraged. It simply shows the value of the exercise. We none of us want or need to be constantly examining what's going on *in here*. But we do need to be sufficiently in touch with it to know what our feelings are when we do decide to take a look. If you're one of those people who often can't come up with an answer, the indications are that you're not very closely in touch with your feelings, for reasons we'll discuss later (page 121). This exercise will help you to put matters right.

If keeping a record every hour proves inconvenient, divide the day up into suitable sessions (morning, afternoon and evening, for example), and at the end of each session analyse how your mood fluctuated during it. At the very least, carry out a review of the day each evening before going to bed. Recall what happened during the day in as much detail as you can – what you did or said, what other people did or said, what went wrong and what went right – and identify the feeling that these events aroused in you, either at the time or when you reflected on them afterwards.

At the weekend, review the record for the whole week. Find a time when you are alone, and can absorb what the record is telling you about yourself. People with family commitments sometimes say that finding time to be alone is impossible. This isn't so – provided your motivation is strong enough. I ask people in this position whether their children can be alone if they wish, whether their partner can. The answer is almost invariably yes. So if the other members of the family have the right to a little privacy, so do you.

Give yourself sufficient time to carry out this weekly review. Insights into yourself come best when your mind is calm and focused. Don't be tempted to skimp things. That way the time you *are* devoting to your review is as good as wasted, and in fact could even produce misleading results. Without proper time for reflection, you can all too easily get a mistaken view of what your record is telling you.

3

HOW YOU BECAME
WHO YOU ARE

A question often asked is, 'Do we inherit our psychological characteristics from our parents and other forebears, or do we acquire them as a result of our experiences in life?' The question is a vitally important one.

The debate about whether we inherit our personality traits, our levels of intelligence and creativity, our talents, our interests, our attitudes and so on from our parents and other forebears, or whether we acquire them as a result of our experiences in life, has been waged with great vigour for many years. The question has crucial implications. If we inherit these states of mind and ways of behaving, then we are very limited in what we can do to prevent them, and ultimately to cope with them. If on the other hand we acquire them as a result of life experiences, then we have much more freedom to do something about them. The debate is much too extensive to enter into here, but it is probably fair to say that few if any of our psychological characteristics depend solely upon inheritance. In other words, no-one is born predestined to become anxious or depressed, no matter what his or her life experiences happen to be.

What we do appear to inherit is our temperament, the raw material which forms the potential from which our personalities, with all their ultimate strengths and weaknesses, will develop, just as we inherit the potential for our physical constitution. Thus, for example, one person may inherit a more placid temperament than another, and this will show up in a tendency to adapt more readily to changes and difficulties in the outside world, and to be more calm and accommodating in behaviour. One person may be temperamentally quicker to anger than another, one person may be more restless, another more sociable, another more affectionate, another more emotional, another more energetic. These differences are very similar to the differences in physical constitution which lead one person to be more resistant to infections than another, or less likely to develop allergies or be affected by harmful chemicals or other forms of environmental pollution.

But if nature gives us our temperament, environment very largely decides how it is going to be developed and used. We come into the world bright with psychological potential in all kinds of ways, but the experiences we receive in life (the encouragements and the discouragements, the opportunities and the lack of opportunities, the advantages and the setbacks) determine just how much of this potential is developed and how much of it is left to go to waste. Thus two people with similar temperaments may develop in very different directions as a result of their different environments, with one leading perhaps a balanced, fulfilled and psychologically happy life, and the other experiencing disappointments, depression and hopelessness.

Of course, it is also true that two people living in similar environments but with very different temperaments will turn out differently. One may come through all kinds of misfortunes and still be psychologically whole, while the same misfortunes may leave the other wrestling with anxieties, frustrations, fears, depressions or any of the other conditions than make our inner lives difficult. But the practical implications of the role played by environment in determining the way our temperaments develop is that our psychological problems aren't programmed into us at conception, and that we therefore do indeed have the power to bring about changes in ourselves.

TEMPERAMENT AND SENSITIVITY

Since our temperament is shaped and moulded by our life experiences from the moment of birth onwards, it's impossible to discern exactly what kind of temperament nature gave you to start with. But studies with babies show that marked differences in temperament are apparent from the early weeks of life, and follow-up studies with the same babies later in childhood and adolescence show that these differences persist to a noticeable extent over the years. Particularly relevant is the fact that some babies appear much more 'nervy' by temperament than others. They are more timid of strangers, less adaptable to new surroundings, more tearful, startle more readily, and have a lower tolerance of hunger, discomfort, and the myriad other inconveniences that temporarily convince a baby that life isn't worth living.

Part of the reason for this nerviness is that such babies have a more 'labile' (I return to the term in a moment) autonomic nervous system than their temperamentally more robust brothers and sisters. The autonomic nervous system is that part of our physiology that handles 'automatic' bodily processes – processes which take place without our having consciously to will them. For the most part it functions separately from our central nervous system, which is involved in thinking and in conscious willing and acting. This distinction between the autonomic and the central nervous system is an important one. An example should help make it clear.

Entering the station to catch a train to Timbuctoo, I see it is about to leave without me. I sprint down the platform, and throw myself, breathless and heart pounding, into the nearest carriage. The realization 'I'm going to miss my train', the decision 'I must run if I am to catch it', and the message to my legs to get moving as fast as they can are all conscious processes, and associated therefore with the central nervous system. But the acceleration in my breathing and in my heart rate which results from my efforts comes about without any conscious action on my part; it is 'switched on' by the autonomic system.

Let's take other examples. My stomach sends me the message that I'm hungry (autonomic nervous system). I decide to look for a restaurant, I find one, I order a meal and I start eating (all central nervous system). The food reaches my stomach and digestion starts (autonomic system). I work hard in the garden all afternoon (central nervous system), my body sends me the message that I am very tired (autonomic system), I decide to go indoors and collapse into an armchair (central nervous system) and within two minutes I have fallen asleep (autonomic nervous system).

Now let's see what this has to do with our psychological problems. Just as it is the autonomic nervous system that speeds up the breathing and the heart rate when we run for a train, and activates the digestive juices when we eat our lunch, and tells us we're tired and puts us to sleep when we've been working in the garden, so it is the autonomic nervous system that activates our emotions in response to our thoughts, or in response to something taking place in the world *out there*. I said in Chapter 2 that there are no magic buttons on our chests that the world *out there* can come and press in order to make us afraid or happy or angry or whatever, and that in the final analysis it is therefore we who do these things to ourselves. The way we do them is through a combination of the central and autonomic nervous systems.

Thus, if you take to thinking about the enjoyable holiday you had last year, and feel happy as a result, it is the combination of your thoughts (central nervous system) and the pleasant emotions they evoke (autonomic nervous system) which is responsible for your happiness. Similarly, if you suddenly see the face of an old friend you haven't met for years, the thought in the central nervous system 'Ah there's so-and-so' triggers the autonomic nervous system into releasing the emotions of pleasure that are associated with being in his company.

On the other hand, if instead of an old friend you see someone whose presence disturbs you, the thought 'Ah there's so-and-so' will trigger the autonomic nervous system into releasing the emotions of anger or fear or apprehension or guilt or whatever it is you currently associate with so-and-so. The autonomic nervous system is therefore very important indeed in human psychology, and as we shall see in due course it is only if we can recognize how it interacts with the central nervous system that we can produce the changes in ourselves which we are seeking, and develop our psychological lives in the way we want, and avoid the arousal of many of our more uncomfortable emotions.

To return now to temperament. It would be wrong in the light of our present knowledge to say that temperament and the autonomic nervous system are one and the same thing, but they are certainly very closely linked to each other.

I said a few moments ago that babies born with what I called a more 'nervy' temperament appear to have a particularly 'labile' autonomic nervous system. What this means is that their autonomic nervous systems are more sensitive than those of other babies, more 'up and down', more subject to extremes. They seem equipped by nature to feel things more deeply. When something threatens them, their autonomic nervous systems are quicker to spring into action. When something disappoints them or frustrates them or pleases them, the same thing happens. This lability tends to persist throughout life, so that they are inclined always to experience life with a particular emotional intensity, an intensity which sends signals back into their central nervous system, thus influencing the way they think about things.

For example, let us suppose they have a threatening experience with a rather fierce dog. The terror this evokes will mean they tend to think fearfully of the dog concerned in the future and, by association, perhaps all dogs. Each time they see a dog, thoughts such as 'There's a dog; it may attack me' will arise, and will lead to further thoughts along the lines of 'I hate dogs'.

By contrast, a person with a less nervy temperament would find that the original experience produced a much less extreme reaction, and in consequence would feel no future fear of dogs, and thus would have more freedom to enjoy them.

No matter what our temperament, the strength of our autonomic responses will of course always be influenced to some extent by past experiences. If I've been badly attacked by dogs in the past, my autonomic nervous system will be more likely to go into a state of alarm when I see a savage-looking specimen coming purposefully in my direction than it otherwise would. But the nature of our temperament can never be ignored. From birth onwards, some people have autonomic nervous systems that are triggered into alarm reactions much more readily and in the face of much smaller threats than others.

We recognize all this when we talk about someone being timid or quick-tempered or affectionate and so on. The recognition of these temperamental tendencies in others helps us to decide how best to relate to them. Equally, in the psychological work we do on ourselves, it helps if we recognize and are true to these tendencies in ourselves. We can't consistently expect calm behaviour from someone who has a mercurial temperament, or stoical courage from someone who alarms easily, or an affectionate response from someone who by nature is rather distant and undemonstrative. Similarly, we can't consistently expect such things from ourselves. To do so is to be unrealistic and attempt to force ourselves into a pattern which clearly doesn't fit, and which, like tight shoes, will go on pinching, restricting and deforming us throughout life.

We have to recognize that the pattern of our emotions – their strength and the speed with which they are activated – is partly determined by our inherited temperament. Equally importantly, we have to recognize that this pattern, like emotions themselves, is psychologically neither good nor bad. It is how we develop it and what we do with it in the face of our life experiences that matters.

THE LIFE SCRIPT

We have reached the point where we can start examining these life experiences and their consequences for the people we are. There are several different ways of doing this (just as there are several different schools of psychology and several different forms of psychological therapies, psychotherapies for short). The method that is most easily understood and put into practice, especially by the person working alone to reshape what goes on *in here*, is to recognize that your life is a form of story, a story which begins at birth and runs throughout your days, and in which you, and nobody else, play the leading character, a character so important that even in sleep you are never off stage, never out of the spotlight.

All around you the scene of the story is constantly shifting and changing. Supporting characters come and go, crises arise and are resolved, there are long steady periods and sudden eruptions into hectic dramatic activity. There are excitements and boring patches, interesting happenings and tedious ones, successes and failures, triumphs and disasters, blessings and tragedies, good times and bad, but throughout it all you remain the constant factor, the one person always at the centre of the action.

If you're about to protest that the 'action' always seems to be somewhere else, that it's always other people who are having the fun and that life passes you by, you're missing the point. In your own particular story, the action always takes place around you. By definition, your story is your own experience of life. It is what happens to you, what you see and hear in the world around you, what you think and feel, what you remember, what you accept and what you reject, what you prize and what you don't prize, what you want and what you don't want, what goes on *in here* while you react with what goes on *out there*.

The baby, the child, the adolescent, the young adult, the mature man or woman, the senior citizen, all these are you. The son or daughter, the only child, the brother or sister, the lover, the husband or wife, the father or mother, the grandparent, all these are you. The schoolchild, the student, the worker, the colleague, the subordinate, the boss. You wear many costumes as you hold centre stage in your story, but it is always you inside the costume, always you experiencing *in here*, always you experiencing the subtle, individual process of being who you are. No-one else can take over your part. No-one else can push you aside, speak your lines for you, carry out your actions.

But – and it is a very big but – if you are the central character in your own story, who is it who *writes the story for you*? Who is responsible for the script? This brings us back to the question in Chapter 1, 'Who is in charge *in here?*' and to the answer, 'Not me'. But it does more than just bring us back. It opens up the broader question of *why* we're not in charge. Is it simply a fact of human life that we exist with little or no say in what goes on inside our mental and emotional lives, our heads and our hearts? Is it simply a fact of human life that we have little or no say in the kind of lives we lead and the way in which we lead and experience them? Is it a fact of human life that the script should always be written for us by someone or something else, and that our psychological problems, which I have already said are not programmed into us at conception, should be there because of the other people and the other things in our lives, and should from the cradle onwards be beyond our own power to change and re-order?

Before we can properly tackle these questions, we need to look more closely at the script and its authors. And to do that, we must go back briefly to the first pages of the script, your early years of life.

How Your Life Script Begins

The term 'life script' is sometimes used in more limited ways by psychologists, but in this book it stands for all those influences that have gone to make you what you are now. These influences are brought to bear upon you from birth onwards, and as we shall see, some understanding of them is essential if you wish to know more about yourself.

You came into the world knowing nothing about it. To the small baby, the world is a new experience, a kaleidoscope of novel sights, sounds and sensations. He or she has nothing to which this experience can be related. No memories, no reference material, no way of asking questions, no sense of logic, no idea of language, of numbers, of colours, of shapes. Everything has to be learnt from scratch.

So total in their novelty were your experiences as a small baby that we have nothing with which we can usefully compare them. It's no good saying it was like an adult being dumped down on the surface of a strange planet. If this happened, at least we'd have some idea of the distinction between animate and inanimate objects, between up and down, between here and there. If intelligent life forms made an appearance, even in the form of little green men and women, we'd have some idea that they might be communicating with each other, whether or not we understood what they were saying. Even in that strange environment, we'd have a host of concepts, of reference points that would help us make some sense of what was going on. Crucially, we would have our own language inside our heads, allowing us to think, to reflect upon experience, to plan and carry out action. And above all, we would have an idea of who *we* are, and of what we need from our environment and from the people and things within it.

As babies we had none of these advantages. We were born with plenty of potential, but with memory banks which were effectively blank. Even if you fancy the idea of reincarnation and of past lives (and the majority of people alive in the world today do so in one form or another) you have to concede that amnesia seems to operate from one life to the next, and the newborn baby starts from scratch.

So where is your life script at birth, and who begins to write it? The answer is, of course, very largely 'other people'. Temperament and other inborn psychological potentials such as our capacity for intelligent thinking, for creativity, for proficiency in music, in the other arts, and in mathematics and science may well determine the number of pages in our script, but the writing that appears on these pages in the early years is put there by other people.

Let's have a look at what this means.

Other people are our first teachers. Long before we can ponder things and begin to make sense of the world for ourselves, other people start teaching us. And these teachers go about their tasks in very different ways. In one household we may learn in the early months of life that when we cry in discomfort, gentle loving hands quickly come to the rescue, and we are picked up and nursed until the world seems a good place again. By contrast, if we live in the next household, we may learn that crying only leads to further discomfort, that nobody comes to the rescue, or only comes brusquely and impatiently.

In one household we may learn that voices speak pleasantly and happily, that they sing songs, and make rhymes. We don't yet understand the words, but the sounds themselves bring happy contact with what is *out there*. In another household, however, we may hear only loud and sudden sounds, or be left for much of the time in silence.

In one we may receive plenty of attention, be played with, and shown colours and shapes that stimulate us to enjoy interacting with *out there*. In another household we may be ignored for most of the time, and only noticed when we scream the place down. In one household we may be helped to feel loved, valued, wanted, while in another we may be left to feel unloved, unwanted, and something of a nuisance.

These are extreme examples, but they help us understand how our early life script is written, and how it will influence what comes later. In one home we may be taught that the world *out there* is a pleasant, caring place, that our attempts to interact with it are welcome, and that all sorts of interesting things are going on within it. In another home we may be taught that *out there* is a pretty formidable and intimidating place, full of things that frighten and upset, and with little in the way of love and support. As the scene *out there* begins to unfold, it influences the unfolding of the scene *in here*. If we're fortunate, *in here* is helped to develop as a happy, contented, interesting place, while if we're less fortunate it may become a confused, stressful and anxious one.

From our early months of life onwards, what is going on *in here* is crucially influenced by what is going on *out there*. The environment may allow us to be more at ease, at peace, at home *in here* than it does the young child next door. And the process rapidly gathers pace as we develop and come more and more to interact with, be aware of, and be influenced by *out there*.

Around the third year of life, much of this crystallizes

further as we acquire a sense of ourself as a separate individual. Up to now, we have been aware of experience, of bodily and emotional sensations, of things happening in the world around, but without being aware of ourself as the experiencer. There has been no real idea of 'me'. But now, with our growing maturity, the idea begins to develop, and with it come all sorts of changes. We come to realize that we can take conscious decisions to do things, to say 'no', to assert our own will, to develop our own ways of doing things. And along with this comes, critically and crucially, the beginnings of self-labelling. Now that we are aware of being 'me', it is possible to become aware of 'me' as a 'good me' or a 'bad me', a 'clever me' or a 'stupid me', a 'nice me' or a 'nasty me'. And where do these self-labels – so important for the life script, both now and afterwards – come from, since we are still too young to choose them for ourselves? From other people, of course.

It is other people (parents, grandparents, aunts, uncles, neighbours, bigger brothers and sisters – and later on schoolteachers) who tell us that we are good or bad, clever or stupid, nice or nasty. And since, when we are small, parents and other big people seem to us to know all there is to know about life, we accept these judgements, and build them into the picture of who we are *in here*. Now that we have acquired language, these labels are given to us verbally ('You *good* boy, Mummy's very pleased with you', 'You *stupid* child, now look what you've done!', 'You *nasty* little girl, I don't know what's got into you'). But they're often backed up with actions. We may be physically handled gently and kindly, or roughly and unfeelingly. We may be guided where our parent wants us to go, or pulled and pushed first here and then there. We may never receive a smack, or we may receive little else.

All these lessons help write the first chapter of the life script. And like any first chapter, this one is vital to what comes afterwards. A first chapter sets the scene for the whole book, rather as the ground plan sets the pattern for the completed building. We can't go back in adult life and rewrite the first chapter, nor can we, in early childhood, influence much of what it is being written within it.

The Early Life Script and Self-Acceptance

From the examples I've just given, you can see that some of us have an early life script that tells us we are valued by the important people in our lives *out there*, and this in turn leads us to value ourselves *in here*. Some of us, by contrast, learn that we have little value and little significance *out there*, and this leads to an equivalent lack of value and significance *in here*. These processes are compounded by the fact that some of us are always sure of our parents' love and care, no matter what happens, while others are given little love or are taught, through threats, that love will be withdrawn if we behave in certain prohibited ways, that love is a conditional thing, likely to be lost at any moment.

The assurance of being loved in these early years, come what may, allows us to see ourselves as lovable human beings, with the result that we are much better able to love ourselves. Loving oneself has nothing to do with conceit, or with thinking how marvellous one is. Conceit and an exaggerated view of our own importance are part of a quite different life script, showing a set of problems of their own to which we need to return later in the book. No, loving oneself really means accepting oneself. We don't need to think of ourself as a marvellous person in order to accept ourself. Like accepting another person, this kind of acceptance is based upon an awareness that we are each of us a mixture of tendencies, some better than others, but that each of us has value as a unique, sentient human being. We don't have to be enormously gifted or wondrously beautiful in order to be worthy of acceptance. We simply have to be human.

It is through acceptance, through being valued for who we are by the important people in our lives – particularly our parents – that we learn this self-acceptance early on. If we are acceptable to them, then surely we must be acceptable to ourselves.

Not only does self-acceptance have nothing to do with conceit, it also has nothing to do with complacency or self-satisfaction, or with a reluctance to change and grow. A loving parent does not think his or her child is perfect. To do so argues self-delusion, which in turn often stems from the insecurity of their own parental love ('I can't love a child who isn't perfect; therefore I must always see *my* child as perfect, whatever he or she does'). Being loved in childhood by a loving parent doesn't give us the mistaken notion we are perfect either. Instead, it gives us the ability to see ourselves as we really are, and to see ourselves as acceptable whatever we are, with all our strengths and weaknesses. It saves us from the life script that says one has to be perfect to be worthy of love.

Self-acceptance allows self-honesty. There is nothing to hide from ourselves. Why should there be? We are not going to hate ourselves for our bad points or despise ourselves for our weaknesses. We are free to see them and accept them for what they are, and by seeing and accepting them in this way, we put ourselves in a better position to change them where change is needed. If I have to go through life pretending to myself that I'm never (or ought never to be) afraid, jealous, envious, angry, tempted, lustful, resentful, then I'm in no position to examine any of these things properly and decide what I should do about them. If I refuse to face up to them, they will remain in place, ready to break out at moments when I've relaxed my inner defences against them, filling me afterwards with regret and self- accusation.

Self-honesty is a vital ingredient in the successful life script. Without it, any attempt to understand and reshape our psychology is virtually impossible. Furthermore, if I can't be honest with myself, I'm unlikely to be honest with anyone else, which in turn renders them less likely to be honest with me, which in turn makes it more difficult to see myself as others see me, which in turn makes it more difficult for me to understand myself. A vicious circle is set up, with the real me confused and lost somewhere in the middle.

SELF-ACCEPTANCE
AND SELF-CONFLICT

One feature often present in our psychological problems is a sense of conflict, either with ourselves or with others. Not the conflict that arises on the one hand from a clear attempt to overcome an aspect of our personalities that we recognize needs changing, or on the other from a legitimate need to oppose what we recognize as unacceptable behaviour in other people, but confused battles that alienate us from part of ourselves or from family, friends and colleagues.

Conflicts of this kind suggest a life script in which parts of our personalities were rejected by others during our formative years, either without proper cause or without proper explanation. In childhood many of us are punished for those very qualities (often temperamental in origin) that society admires most in adults. Determination, for example, strength of will and of purpose, outspokenness, initiative, honesty, individuality, curiosity, energy and enthusiasm – many of the qualities, in short, which will one day stand us in good stead, but which for the moment are inconvenient to the adults in our world, who end up not only condemning them but giving us the idea that we are 'bad' to possess them.

All too often this condemnation stays with us when we are grown-up, leaving us still fighting an inner battle against what we have been taught to see as the negative side of our nature. Only by realizing the inappropriateness of this state of affairs are we able to bring this inner conflict to an end and get to know and accept ourselves more fully, and put ourselves in a position to make better use of our potential.

This doesn't mean, of course, that there are no aspects of ourselves we need to deal with. Social living necessarily requires that we learn to give as well as to take, that we study the needs of others as well as of ourselves, and that we learn how to express our emotions in ways that do not cause unnecessary suffering to those around us or to ourselves. This can mean a hard struggle at times. But such a struggle is best carried out from a position of understanding – the understanding that comes from being taught, at the time when we were first learning them, *why* socially acceptable behaviours are important, and why we should learn to accommodate them. Without this teaching, we may still, even in adult life, be rebelling against these behaviours as unnecessary restraints upon our freedom, or following them out of unthinking obedience. Either way, we deny ourselves the opportunity to *own* our own behaviour more fully, and to put ourselves in a better position to appraise it properly and take decisions on the direction our future change and development should take.

The Early Life Script and Emotions

Acceptance by parents and others close to us is crucial in the writing of the opening chapter of our life script. But it is not enough for parents simply to tell a child that they love him or her, and always will. Important as verbal assurances of love certainly are, more is needed.

In the first years of our lives, we lived very much in and through our emotions. Not yet able to reason things out or to reflect fully upon experience, our behaviour was very much a reflection of how we felt. Outbursts of joy, of temper, of jealousy, of distress, of disappointment were never far from the surface. As young children, we had very little control over these impulses, or over the actions that accompanied them. So in the early years we didn't have free choice over whether to be 'naughty', or a 'nuisance' or even 'good'. The emotion came to the surface, and we acted.

Of course adults often objected to our emotional outbursts, and we ended up blamed sometimes for the simple fact that we were emotional human beings. Of course we had to learn the restraints necessary for social living, but there is a major difference between accepting that our emotions are natural and acceptable in themselves and helping us learn to control and use them properly, as a loving parent does, and punishing us simply for having these emotions.

The former, constructive, way of relating to children

involves guiding their actions without rejecting them as
people. It allows them to recognize that emotions are part
of being human, and that one has no need to feel guilty
or ashamed for their existence. The latter, negative, way
leaves them feeling that there is something wicked about
certain emotions (for example fear in boys, aggression in
girls), and that these emotions lurk inside them just waiting
to prove to the world what bad little boys or girls they
are.

Other Barriers to Self-Acceptance

Rejecting part of our emotional life was one way in which
people gave us negative self-images when we were children,
and came between us and self-acceptance. But there were
other ways. For example, we may have been given a limited
sense of personal significance because adults always seemed
too busy to spend much time with us, or because we
sensed they attached little importance to our ideas and
our wishes. Or older people may have been physically
violent towards us, giving us the impression that our
bodies were there primarily to be punished and to be
made to feel physical pain. Or we may have been given
the idea that other children in the family or in the class
at school were always favoured above us and compared
with us to our disadvantage. Any or all of these things
will have contributed to make us question our value and
our right to the high esteem of others and therefore of
ourselves, and may well have left us, dependent upon
our temperaments, struggling with low self-confidence or
looking to build ourselves up with exaggeratedly aggressive
and self-assertive behaviour.

Another disadvantage we may have experienced is an
inconsistent background, the kind of background in which
people treat us well one day and then, for no apparent
reason, badly the next. The effect of this upon us in our
formative years, when we are busy learning the ways of
the world, is to leave us confused not only about other
people but also about ourselves, since we inevitably feel

that it must be something in *us* that is responsible for their changes of mood, though we've no idea what it can possibly be.

Think how confusing it would be if physical phenomena behaved in the same unpredictable way: if water made us wet one day and dry the next, if fire was hot one minute and cold the next, if food satisfied us at one meal and made us hungry at the next. The resulting confusion would leave us feeling very insecure, especially if it appeared to us that it was some action or actions on our part that was to blame.

Inconsistency is also seen in what psychologists call the *double-bind*, the situation in which, whatever someone does, he or she loses. For example, a child is punished for being noisy, and shortly afterwards accused of sulking when they try to keep quiet. Or a child is pushed aside and told not to be silly when they offer physical affection, and the next day accused of not being loving enough when they try to show restraint. Frequent experience of the double-bind makes us doubt ourselves and find it hard to trust others, and it is the ability to trust that gives us the security and confidence to reach out and explore the world, and relate to other people without unwonted suspicion or doubt.

Self-doubt can also result if we are *invalidated* by adults during our formative years; that is, when our ideas and opinions and the statements we make about ourselves are frequently contradicted by them. It isn't easy to believe in ourselves and in what we think and in how we feel when our attempts to put these things into words are constantly being contradicted by people who supposedly know more about life than we do.

If all this sounds rather negative, take heart! There are very few of us without disadvantages of some kind in our background, and the good news is that, tackled through techniques such as those discussed in this book, these disadvantages can not only be overcome, but can actively help us in our personal growth. It is indeed through overcoming them that we learn to build our psychological strength, and to develop the ability to give the right help and support to others when they are in need.

Sex Roles

Another important influence on the early life script is whether we're born male or female. Research shows that parents tend to treat boys and girls differently from the early weeks of life onwards. This is not simply a case of blue for a boy and pink for a girl. Girl babies and toddlers are picked up and comforted more than boys, while boys are encouraged to be more independent and adventurous. Boisterous, noisy activity is more tolerated in small boys than in small girls, and once they learn to walk, small boys are generally allowed to wander farther from their parents while at play than small girls, to spend more time outside the home, and to be excused as they grow older from work in the kitchen and from other domestic chores.

If you're a girl, the chances are you were actively discouraged from engaging in the physical aggression tolerated and even rewarded in boys, and from developing the more assertive side of your nature. As you grew older there was less encouragement and less opportunity for you to participate in sport, to take part-time jobs outside the home, to go on adventurous outings and holidays, to take an interest in DIY projects, and to learn to use hand tools. Judged by recent evidence, you were probably also less encouraged to use computers, to take an interest in information technology, and generally to become familiar with the electronic revolution.

Where boys and girls mix together, boys are generally expected to take the lead and outshine the girls, an expectation that becomes more and more obvious as children grow older. An able girl will even tend to depress her performance when paired with a less able boy in a task involving skill of some kind, while a more able boy paired with a less able girl will maintain or even boost his. Research suggests that when the sexes take part in joint ventures, boys and men receive two-thirds of the good things that are going (praise, prestige, prizes,

salary, attention – even active roles in group discussions)
while girls and women have to be content with one
third.

On the other hand, if you're a boy, you were in all
probability denied the freedom given to girls to show the
gentler side of your nature, to express your fears, to cry,
and to ask for help. Nor in all probability did you spend so
much time with adults, with all the advantages this brings
for the development of language skills and of maturity that
being with adults entails.

Thus in different ways, whether you are a girl or a
boy, you were limited by the sexual stereotyping that
goes on in the early pages of the life script (and which
continues throughout life). Ways of exploring yourself and
your relationships with others, of being in touch with your
emotions, or developing your interests and ambitions were all
hindered for you in different ways, depending on your sex.

By its denial of equal opportunities, sexual stereotyping
can limit the development of our full psychological
maturity. A characteristic of this maturity is a rounded
and well-balanced personality. The exaggeratedly macho
and dominant male, the exaggeratedly non-macho and
defenceless female, both hint strongly at one-sided development. Biological factors (including temperament) dictate
that certain differences in outlook, interests and behaviour
between males and females are always likely to remain, but
the humanity shared by us all is much more important than
the differences dictated by our gender. We each of us carry
male and female inside us, and psychological wholeness
demands we be in contact with both aspects of ourselves
and give them their proper chance to develop and find means
of expression.

MORE ABOUT SEX ROLES

Figures show that psychological problems are more commonly
reported among women than men. Women consult the
doctor more often about depression, anxiety, insomnia and

other related psychological disorders, and are more likely
to need specialist psychiatric help for mental illness. (One
woman in eight will be given such help at some point in her
life as opposed to one man in twelve.)

Why is this? Are women really the 'weaker' sex when
it comes to psychological difficulties? We don't know for
sure. But there's a strong likelihood that sex roles play
an important part. There are a number of reasons for
this.

1. Women face far greater conflict between the demands
    of family and the demands of career than men, a point
    to which I return when discussing the case of Julia in
    Chapters 4 and 8.

2. In career terms, women have much less chance of
    fulfilment than men. In almost all walks of life, due
    primarily to lack of opportunity, they occupy lower-
    paid, more monotonous, and lower-status jobs than
    men.

3. Women have less personal power in their lives: less say
    over what they want to do, where they want to live,
    what career they want to follow, even over how they
    want to spend their leisure time.

4. Women have more emotional demands made upon
    them and upon their time. It is women who look
    after the children, who look after the sick, who look
    after the elderly, who care for ailing parents.

5. Women are more likely to be more socially isolated than
    men, spending their days with young children at home,
    cut off from social contact with the outside world.

6. Women are generally under more pressure to be con-
    formist than men, to put others before self, to know
    their 'place', to put up with things, to keep the peace,

to listen to other people's problems, to act as the 'glue' that holds society together – and they receive inadequate recognition for their efforts.

Any and all of these reasons may be enough to explain why women are more likely to need psychological help than men. But there is another, much more subtle but equally important, reason. That is that psychological health is largely defined in male terms. The psychologically healthy person is supposed to be rational, self-controlled, to know what he or she wants, to be able to stand up for him or herself, to be tough, resilient, and self-sufficient. Many of these are either things which go against the feminine temperament or things which women are taught by their sex roles expressly *not* to be or do. Add to this the fact that most doctors and psychiatrists are men, and therefore – however dedicated and compassionate – not always well-suited to understanding the female predicament, and you have some comprehensive reasons for why there are more women than men either with, or diagnosed as having, psychological problems.

Birth Order

A less obvious but still important early influence upon the life script is birth order. Parents frequently say they're less relaxed with their first child than with second and subsequent ones. First children may also have more demanded of them later, as the oldest and most responsible child, and they will certainly experience the pangs of jealousy when a younger brother or sister arrives, and the pangs of impatience and injustice when the younger child interferes with their play and is protected from retaliation by parents.

On the other hand, if you're a first child you will have had an early and powerful experience of being biggest and best at everything, of being the leader, and of being trusted and put in charge. You may also have been taught to grow up more quickly than your younger brothers and sisters (which has its good and bad sides), and may have learnt earlier than them the lessons of independence and initiative.

By contrast, younger or youngest children grow up with the threat of inferiority. If you're a younger or youngest child you will have had bigger brothers and sisters who could do the things and be allowed to try the things you could not. By way of compensation however, you will have had the guidance, the protection and the stimulation provided by your older siblings. And assuming that you were not treated as the baby of the family for too long – and learnt in consequence that the best way to get what you wanted was to feign helplessness or scream very loud – you will have benefited in terms of accelerated learning and maturity.

If you're a middle child, you will have faced a different situation again. The risk for middle children is that they may miss out on the kind of attention received by both the oldest and the youngest child. The oldest child is an only child in the months or years before the second child is born, and the youngest child is also an 'only' child during the months or years when siblings are at school and he or she is still at home. As a middle child, you may therefore never have spent as much time alone with adults (with the physical affection and mental stimulation this can bring) as the other children in your family, and may have had to fend more for yourself.

If you're an only-child, you will have faced yet another different situation. Though benefiting from more adult attention, you would have been denied the companionship of brothers and sisters. You may also have been over-protected, or have had too much expected of you, or, like the youngest child in a family, been kept a baby for too long, with the consequences just mentioned.

Other aspects of the family set-up that influence the life script, for better or worse, are such things as having very young and inexperienced parents; having parents who are significantly older than the norm; belonging to a family that moves house a great deal and fails to give you a chance to experience the security of friends and familiar surroundings; belonging to a one-parent family, or to a close extended family which gives you lots of social contact with uncles and aunts and grandparents and cousins.

Minority Groups

If you are a member of a minority group in society, this can also lead to problems in the life script. By the simple fact of being 'different' from others, you can find yourself ostracized, discriminated against, and with a sizeable inferiority complex as a result. This is true for people with a noticeable physical or mental disability, for people who are more creative (and therefore often less conformist) than others, for people who are markedly shorter or taller, for people who are frailer, who are more attracted sexually to their own than to the opposite sex, even for people who are markedly more intelligent or gifted in some way than their peers.

But perhaps nowhere is this more true than for ethnic minority groups. If you are black or coloured, this can often mean that you are handed a life script which labels you, not in terms of ability, personality, or any of the other things that make up who you really are, but simply in terms of the pigment in your skin.

Looked at objectively, few things could be more absurd. For reasons that have nothing to do with your real worth, such a life script may virtually dictate where you live, where you go to school, who in later life you are likely to marry, and what kind of opportunities and careers will be fully open to you. The effect of a life script of this kind can be to leave you feeling inadequate about yourself on the one hand, or bitter and hostile towards the world on the other. Both responses – and the various gradations in between – can profoundly influence both your self-image and your philosophy of life.

Starting School: The Life Script Continues

By the time you started school, your life script was already a bulky document, telling you what you could and could not do, what feelings were acceptable and what weren't, how you should and should not use language, how you should relate to others, how you should treat your physical surroundings, the extent of your power over your own life, and what the significant people around you thought of you and felt towards you.

Above all, your life script told you who you were; that is, how you should see yourself, think about yourself, judge yourself and experience your own being. Whether this picture of yourself was the 'right' one or not is quite another matter. The important thing is that you had no other. You took over this self-image lock stock and barrel, believed in it, and came to think, feel and act in accordance with it.

Once school started, the second chapter opened in your life script, often reinforcing much of what was written in chapter one. The characteristic pattern of behaving that you learnt in chapter one of the script was carried over into school, and the teacher's response to you was influenced by it. If the teacher liked the pattern, he or she tended to see you favourably. If he or she disliked it, the opposite was the case. Just to confuse matters for you, he or she may have responded unfavourably to things that you had been encouraged to do at home, and may have encouraged things that at home were forbidden.

For example, at home you may have been called 'good' for showing initiative, for speaking up, for questioning and debating. At school, these things may have been frowned on, leaving you feeling that these were the qualities that labelled one a 'nuisance'. Alternatively you may have been called 'good' at home for keeping quiet, saying little and generally keeping as low a profile as possible. At school, such behaviour may have been labelled 'withdrawn', and you may have found yourself pushed reluctantly into social activities by the teacher.

Or if you were a child who had been taught that good little children are those who are polite, ask nicely for what they want, and wait their turn, you may now have found that this behaviour was a sure way of ensuring that you never got a turn at anything. Conversely, if you had learnt at home that the only way to get what you wanted was to grab it first and hold on to it against all comers, you may now have found that this was the one way to ensure you ended up with nothing.

Starting school was a traumatic experience for most of us, no matter how good the school and no matter how adaptable we happened to be. Having learnt chapter one of our life script of home, we were faced with what was often a quite different script, introducing a quite different plot, vocabulary and even grammar. Like trying to make sense of a book where vital pages linking one chapter to the next are missing, we frequently had to struggle with this new life script in which there were new script writers with new ideas on what the main story line should and should not be.

The Experience of Success and Failure

One of the most important features of this new story line was the experience of success and failure. You would already have been introduced to this experience in the home, but once at school its impact would have been multiplied many times over, because at school there were formal measures of success and failure to be contended with, such as teacher approval and disapproval and – all too soon – ticks and crosses, star charts, house points, and teacher's red ink. There were also other children with whom your performance was compared, and parental pleasure and displeasure at your 'progress' or lack of it, and at the teacher's comments about you.

The experience of success and failure rapidly added page after page to chapter two of your life script. We have a need for success in childhood and throughout life because it brings with it the praise, status, and prestige that help build our belief in ourselves as effective human beings, and that prompt us to go on and make full use of our potential. It continues the process begun in chapter one of marking us out as worthwhile members of the community, with some control over our environment and over aspects of our own destiny. Above all, it helps build our self-esteem and our respect for our abilities, and helps us identify appropriate standards and goals for the future.

Failure, on the other hand – particularly repeated failure or sudden unexpected failure – has the opposite effect. It leads others to reduce the value they place upon us. It lowers our horizons, limits our ambitions, reduces our prospects in life and the expectations we have of ourselves. And naturally it lowers our self-esteem, leads us to revise downwards the picture of who we think we are, and to feel negatively rather than positively about ourselves and our place in the scheme of things.

Consistent failure in our childhood years blots the life script, and reduces the importance in the eyes of others of our role in the world. It breeds in us a sense of inferiority from which we may have to struggle to break free for the rest of our life. At no time should we ever underestimate its adverse and long-term consequences.

Your Response to Failure

Both in our early lives and later on, we respond in different ways to failure, depending upon temperament and upon whether we have learnt in chapter one of our life script to respect or reject authority. Some people become accepting and hopeless: 'I'm no good at anything and I never will be any good.' They blame themselves for their failure, and see the judgements passed on them by teachers and those in authority over them as no more than they 'deserve'. Other people become resentful and hostile. The failure is seen as the fault of others: 'I could do the work if I wanted to, but it's boring/stupid/a waste of time'. Yet others blame bad luck, or lack of opportunity, or the privileges which they regard as extended to others but denied to them. A few – a very few – are stimulated and challenged by failure, and determine at all costs to prove to the world what they really can do in life.

Whatever the response, it becomes written into the life script under the heading 'The Person I Am'. It becomes a vital part of the way in which we see ourselves, and determines much of the way in which we react to others and to ourselves, and much of the way in which we plan and prepare for the future. It is instrumental in determining the kind of qualifications with which we leave school, the kind of jobs we obtain, our prospects for advancement, the salaries we earn, and ultimately the sense of achievement and of personal fulfilment we get from life.

Success or failure are not confined in chapter two of the script to how well or how badly we do at school. They are also experienced in our social relationships; in, for example, our popularity with other children, the ease with which we make friends, the kind of people who like us, and our success with the adults we meet. Success and failure are also experienced in the way in which others respond to us physically (individuals with high levels of self-esteem tend to come from homes with plenty of the physical affection that reassures us that we're nice to be near), in the way in which they admire or criticize our clothes and our looks, and in the extent to which they pay us attention. In short, success and failure are experienced in the degree of social value others place upon us.

This isn't the end of the story. Success and failure are also a consequence of the way other people apply their standards. If we did well at school, but never well enough to satisfy an over-demanding parent, we were in a sense experiencing failure in the midst of actual success. So were we if we were brought up in an inconsistent environment, and never allowed to know exactly what the standards expected of us actually were. So were we if we felt our family compared unfavourably in socio-economic status with the families of our friends, or if we had over-protective parents and were left friendless by not being allowed to mix with others or to choose our own companions.

Failure over a long period, whatever the cause, leaves us feeling diminished in our early years, and this feeling can persist into adult life. Like a building with uncertain foundations, we are left unsure of ourselves. The result can be a generalized inferiority complex that leaves us convinced that what we have to offer life is never quite good enough, and leaves us feeling that we want to apologize in some sense for being who we are, and that others are more able and gifted than we.

The Influence of Culture

A final influence upon the life script is our culture. One aspect of this was mentioned when I talked earlier about the different roles assigned to males and females. These roles are in large part culturally determined. It is our culture that gives traditional roles to men and women, and it is our culture that exerts the pressures on us to remain within these roles.

But culture does much more than this. It is our culture that decides what counts as success and failure in life. If you doubt this, compare the fact that as much adulation is given to a pop star in the West as is given to a holy man or woman in parts of the East. It is our culture that teaches us what to prize (largely money and possessions in the West), what moral standards to apply (all is fair in politics and business), what clothes are fashionable, what sports are catered for, what jobs and professions are open to us, and what we can do with our leisure time. It also dictates what religion we should follow if we don't want to be regarded as cranks, what illnesses we are likely to have, what social class we occupy, what our life expectancy is, what charities and political parties are available, what kinds of behaviour in us or in anyone else qualify as abnormal, and what attitudes we are likely to have towards the rest of the world.

Much of this is communicated to us, not through legal sanctions, but through unwritten codes of conduct, through the history and geography of our nation, and through the messages carried by the media. To be British or American is to have quite different entries in our script than to be African or Chinese. Many of the entries are not necessarily 'right' or 'wrong'. They are simply different from one culture to the next, and they exert a profound influence over us throughout life. Each culture demands and expects different things of those who belong to it, gives them different opportunities, and prompts them to develop different identities and different ways of looking at and feeling about life.

Over and above these general factors, our culture affects

each one of us in an intensely personal way. It puts into our hands certain books, music, pictures and other outpourings from the media and creative arts. At the touch of a radio or TV button it gives us access to the varied and wonderful offerings of this and previous centuries. It is impossible to overestimate the importance to the life script of the books we read from early years onwards, of the music we hear and the pictures we see, and of the material that comes to us over the airwaves.

To take just the example of books, many of us can testify to the lasting influence upon our young minds of the stories and the poems that we read in childhood. Our heroes and our villains, our adventures, our joys and disappointments, our concepts of good and bad, of honour and of dishonour, our ideas of other places and other realities, our dreams and our ambitions, even our ideas about ourselves, were influenced by the books we curled up with in a corner. For many of us, these books were in fact one of the most formative – not to say magical – experiences of our early years.

Some of us were given more opportunities to benefit from what is best in our culture than others. We were given more in the way of books, and more peace and quiet in which to enjoy them. We were taken to the theatre, taken on educational visits, given music lessons, and provided with guidance, encouragement and approval in our cultural interests. Others of us grew up in a less advantaged environment, and may have been denied the chances properly to explore our own imagination through creative experiences. These factors, together with the other cultural ones I've mentioned, made further entries in our life scripts, helping to influence the chapters that followed.

REVIEWING YOUR EARLY LIFE SCRIPT

I have now detailed many of the ways in which the early chapters of your life script have come to be written. In your own case, there will have been other important experiences that I haven't been able to cover, but the outline I've given

should help you to look back at your early years and see
something of the way in which it helped form the person
you are. The following exercise will help you to reflect on
this outline in more detail.

▶ **Exercise 8: Looking at your early life script**

1. Describe what you regard as your temperament
   in a sentence or two. Do you feel for example
   that by nature you are extroverted, sociable and
   outgoing, or introverted and more concerned with
   your inner states of mind? Would you say you are
   naturally rather anxious and nervy, or naturally
   calm and unruffled? Are you affectionate by nature,
   or inclined to be physically a little distant? Are you
   naturally cheerful, or a little on the low-spirited
   side? Are you naturally strong-willed, determined
   and outspoken, or more passive and retiring?

2. Now consider the extent to which you feel your
   life script has allowed you to be true to your
   temperament. Do you feel that certain parts of it have
   been curbed and frustrated, or that generally you are
   what your temperament intended you to be?

3. Do you feel you are in touch with your feelings –
   that is, do you feel in touch with your emotional
   life, and that you can accept it and, where you feel
   this is the right thing to do, express it?

4. Can you be honest with yourself about the way you
   are, or do you tend to hide things from yourself? If
   you do hide things, can you say why you do this?

5. Do you feel in harmony with yourself, or are certain
   parts of you in conflict with other parts? If such a
   conflict exists, what is the cause? Is part of you
   victimizing or constantly criticizing another part?
   If so, what is the source of this victimization or
   criticism? Is it as if you have an internalized parent
   or teacher who is still controlling you and writing
   your script for you?

6. Did the important adults in your life seem to have time for you when you were growing up, or did you feel you had constantly to be finding ways of attracting their attention? If you were short of attention, what effect has this had upon you?

7. Were people for the most part consistent in their dealings with you, so that you gained a clear picture of what they were like and how you could best relate to them, or did you often feel confused and unsure of how they were going to react to you?

8. Were you clear what was wanted of you, or were you sometimes in the double-bind of being wrong whatever you did? Were you usually able to express your real thoughts and feelings, or did it seem that you were often invalidated so that you ended up confused and uncertain about yourself?

9. Did you find it and do you still find it easy to trust others? To trust yourself? If not, can you identify why?

10. What was it like to be a boy or a girl in your family and in your school? Did you feel restricted by your sex role? Did you envy the other sex? If you answer 'yes' to these questions, what is the lasting effect that your sex role has had upon you?

11. If you had brothers and sisters, what was your position in the family? What effect did being the oldest or the youngest or a middle child have upon you? If you were an only-child, what effect did this have?

12. If you are a member of an ethnic or cultural minority, how has this influenced your life script? How has it influenced the way you feel about yourself and others? How has it influenced the opportunities you had and expect to have in life?

13. What effect did your school years have upon you?

Can you still remember starting school? What kind of experience was it? What was your relationship with your teachers, and what values did you learn from school? To what extent were these values in agreement or in conflict with the ones you learnt at home?

14. Has your life script up to now been characterized by the experience of success or failure? Give the answer less in terms of what you have actually achieved than in terms of how others have made you feel about yourself.

15. What influence has the culture in which you were raised had upon you? Think in terms of the standards, values and fashions of your country and of your social and/or ethnic group. Think in terms of the access you have been given to books, to the arts, to science, and to the media, and try to gauge what you have learnt as a consequence.

Use the answers to these questions as food for thought and as a way towards greater self-understanding. But when looking back at your past in this way, there are three important things to keep always in mind.

1. Don't look back in regret, identifying the things that went wrong and wishing they had been different. We can't alter the past, and it's a waste of time to brood over it. But we can alter many of the *consequences* of the past, and that is what this book is about.

2. Don't look back in bitterness. You may see clearly the authors who were responsible for some of the undesirable pages in your script, but they were human beings like the rest of us, whose behaviour was influenced in turn by the undesirable pages others wrote for them. They had their own problems, as I stressed in Chapter 1, and may well have been unaware that they were passing these problems on to you.

3. Look back with the intention of learning. Identifying
    the mistakes that were written into the early chapters of
    your script doesn't automatically remove the problems
    these mistakes have caused, but it does help you to
    see where these problems came from, and thus to put
    yourself in a much better position to recognize the right
    way of dealing with them.

There is an old saying that he (or she) who forgets the past
is condemned to repeat it. Such a saying can be interpreted
at a number of different levels, but for us it emphasizes the
value of remembering and understanding what has gone to
make us the people we are. Writers of autobiography stress
a similar point when they affirm the priceless value to their
present lives of recalling and reflecting upon the years that
have gone before.

   We none of us can repeat our past years, of course, and
change whatever we dislike about them. But we can do
something better. We can stop ourselves repeating the script
they wrote for us. Remembering the past can be a painful
experience at times, but ultimately it is a liberating one,
since it helps us to see that many of the things we would
like to change in our present-day selves have been put there
by something extrinsic to ourselves. And since they were
put there by our experience, are learnt rather than inherited,
it is open to us now to learn how to overcome them.

4

OTHER PEOPLE AND YOU

In the last chapter we saw that we bring into the world our temperament, the raw material for the people we are, but that it is our environment from birth onwards that starts to write our life script and determines how that temperament will be developed and the kind of person we will become. In this chapter we are going to examine not only the ways in which other people continue to influence your life script through into adult life, but also how you can begin to take more control over what happens *in here*. This means changing the way in which you think and feel about yourself, the way in which you see yourself in relation to others and to the world *out there*, and the way in which you perceive your abilities and the meaning your life has for you. Let's pick up the story in your adolescent years.

ADOLESCENCE TO ADULTHOOD

Adolescence is a vital chapter in your life script, because it is during the adolescent years that you began the transition from a child to a grown-up. Your early years had taught you how to cope with childhood; now you were faced with a whole new set of lessons: how to manage in the much bigger, less personal, more complex world of the adult. In the West, there is a sharp divide between childhood and adulthood. Children have few rights, adults have many. Children are dependent, adults are independent. Children have little say over what they do with their lives, adults (in theory at least) have a great deal.

The abruptness of this move from dependence to

independence can bring with it many difficulties. Having learnt what your life script expected of you in childhood and what standards and values it sought to teach, you are suddenly on the brink of an adult life with a different set of criteria which will demand that you take your own decisions, choose your own relationships, make your own way in the world. Western society, unlike many less 'developed' communities, provides no proper transitional stage during these years which allows the child to work alongside adults and be gradually initiated into their world. Instead there are the uneasy adolescent years, when the individual is no longer biologically a child and yet not socially an adult.

The storms and trials of adolescence are thus in many ways a consequence of our Western culture, symptoms of the adolescent's attempt to acquire what is essentially a new identity – that of an adult – but with very variable guidance and support on how this should be done.

However, simply because we were on the brink of adulthood didn't mean we were left to write our own scripts. Other authors still played a major role. In our adolescent search for a new identity, much of what most of us did was experimental. We tried out first one set of attitudes and behaviours and then another, rather as a person tries on new clothes to see which look best. But it was often other people who decided for us what was suitable and what was not. Many of these sets of attitudes and behaviours had to be discarded therefore – for example because they didn't fit in with our peer group or because they led to too much conflict with our elders or because we were left in no doubt that they would be unacceptable to future employers. Our adolescent years were thus, in their own way, still restricted by the script writers at our elbows.

Some of the guidance we were given was helpful, of course, and essential to us if we were to learn about the wider world we were soon to enter. But the point to remember is that once more our freedom was limited. At times we were given wise counsel that helped us reflect upon our lives and make sensible and informed decisions about who and what we wanted to be. At times we were

given the space to find our own independence and the
personal and social responsibilities that go with it. But
at other times there is a good chance we were left with
the feeling that we were being asked to put on a suit that
didn't fit, and to become someone we were convinced we
were not.

ADULTHOOD

Once you became an adult, your script was still often in
the hands of others. Employers and colleagues, with their
demands and expectations, wrote several pages of it. Work
can sometimes force us to adopt one identity (with its own
set of values, standards and behaviours) in the office and
quite another at home. For the fortunate, the two identities
may be compatible, but those of us who are unfortunate
may have to fit ourselves into an irksome, artificial and
demanding straitjacket each morning, which leaves us
feeling stiff and uncomfortable when it is discarded at the
end of the working day. For example, we may find ourselves
having to espouse values of toughness, even ruthlessness
at work, while at home we are expected to be gentle and
understanding. Or at work we may have to be quiet and
introverted, and at home lively and extroverted.

Straitjacket or no straitjacket, working in any job gives us
an identity in and of itself. Notice how in English we use
the verb 'to be', the verb that proclaims our very existence,
when we are describing our occupation. 'I am a teacher,'
we say, or 'I am a carpenter', or 'I am a housewife' or a
bricklayer or a solicitor or an office cleaner or a secretary
or a salesperson or an airline pilot. We don't say 'I work at'
these occupations. We say 'I am' them. 'I am a teacher' and
'I am me' carry the same grammatical power as each other,
and therefore express how closely identified we are with our
occupation.

Further proof of this strong identification with job or
profession comes from the reaction many people have when
suddenly put out of work, or when they retire, or even

when they are promoted, or moved sideways, or change occupations voluntarily. However much they may feel they were separate from their job, they often suffer a long period of readjustment during which they endeavour to seek a new identity, a period in which they feel curiously anonymous and ineffectual, without that clear sense of 'who I am' that characterized them while in their former job.

If you find yourself in this position, the people around you may make your readjustment even more difficult, since they also no longer identify you with your work. In consequence they may now view you as less powerful, less significant. Like it or not, our occupation plays for most of us a major role in our lives, and is responsible for some very important entries in our life script.

Our culture also makes entries in that as an adult it expects you to abide by its laws. To be a respectable citizen you have to pay your taxes, avoid certain drugs, wear clothes in public, give various items of information about yourself and your circumstances on demand, avoid crime, bankruptcy and breaches of the peace, and generally act as a responsible and reliable member of the community.

These restrictions, necessary as they for the most part are, have a powerful effect on identity. A conviction for even a minor civil offence can upset someone for months afterwards, not because of the punishment involved, which is often trivial, but because the new role of law-breaker has now to be incorporated into their identity, changing the picture they have of themselves.

Family

The most vital element in our life script for most of us, however, remains the family. The family provides the major social context of our lives. It is the family (parents and siblings, and later partner and children) that is chiefly responsible for emotionally supporting us, moulding us, and in some cases even helping to destroy us (psychologically if not physically). Let's look first at the family relationship of husband and wife, or of two partners.

If you're in a relationship, you're probably aware that it involves compromise. The closer the relationship, the more compromise may be needed. For two people to live together successfully, they must adapt to each other. In the process of this adaptation, you and your partner have to discard or keep in abeyance certain things about yourselves. In effect, each of you has to give something of yourself to the other. It may be quite small things, like keeping silent about your annoyance with each other's personal habits, or with behaviours like lateness or untidiness. Minor though these things may seem, each time you make allowance for them you are giving up that part of yourself that wants others always to be free of such habits or to be on time or to be tidy. You may also be giving up the anger you want to express, or the desire to get back at your partner by deliberately doing things which he or she is known to dislike.

This is even more so in the case of major issues. There may be serious personality differences between you and your partner, or fundamental disagreements about money, or about whether to have children, or about how to bring them up, or about whether extra-marital affairs are acceptable, or about how to relate to in-laws, or about whether to move house or to change a job or to believe in God. Such matters can often only be resolved by major compromise, or by capitulation on the part of one or other partner. Such compromise or capitulation may even extend to staying with the partner instead of moving out, or to giving up an extra-marital relationship, or to remaining childless when one yearns for parenthood.

Traditionally (and unfairly) it is more often the female partner who compromises or capitulates, but whoever does so, it means giving up a significant part of the self. Control over a major area of the life script is put in the hands of someone else, even if the decision to compromise is made through justifiable concern for the wellbeing of the other person, for their happiness, or for their fulfilment in life. The results for oneself need not be negative. Through self-sacrifice we can often add an important new dimension to ourselves. But if we are to do so, we need usually to feel that our efforts are appreciated and that they are made voluntarily, rather than expected of us and taken for granted.

The arrival of children puts further pages of your script in the hands of others. In the last chapter I discussed how your parents wrote much of the early chapters of your life script for you. Now it's time to make clear that the process works both ways. Children write much of the life script for their parents too. Initially they do this unwittingly. Their dependence means that as a parent you have to subordinate much of yourself to your children – the pattern of your days, your financial planning, your time and energy, your thoughts, your fears, your hopes and your expectations. (See my book *Your Growing Child*, Fontana 1990, for further explanation.)

As children grow older, their part in writing your life script becomes more conscious. They begin to make intentional demands – for affection, for time, for guidance, for space, for money. They come to recognize your weak points, how to get round you in order to obtain what they want, how to manipulate, how to make you feel guilty and inadequate. None of this is bad in itself. Children have very little power as of right over their own lives and the lives of others, as we saw in the last chapter, and it is both understandable and legitimate that they should discover ways of using what little power they have. But once again, the result is a further restriction upon who you are and upon what you can do with your life. Women usually bear the main burden of this restriction. It affects their lives both inside and outside the home, and does so, moreover, during the years when they are at their most energetic and creative. Julia's case history is a good example of this.

JULIA: RESTRICTIONS OF HOME AND FAMILY
The mother of three small children, one of whom has not yet started school, Julia is fortunate in that she and her husband Tom have a reasonable income from his work as a surveyor, and are able to live in a pleasant house with plenty of space for the children to live and grow. However, when I saw Julia she described herself as 'in despair most of the time'. Much as she loved her children and her husband,

she felt herself losing any sense of, as she put it, 'where I end and the rest of the family begin'.

Her time, her thoughts, her energy were being constantly siphoned off into Tom and the children. 'I have to be who they want me to be, never who I want to be. In fact it's got so that I don't know any more who I *do* want to be. I just sort of exist somewhere in the middle of getting Tom and the children off in the mornings, cleaning the house, washing and ironing clothes, shopping, making meals, sorting out the children's endless fights, listening to their tales, listening to the problems Tom brings home from work, and generally acting as a sort of litter bin into which everyone else stuffs their rubbish.'

Before her first child, Julia worked as a commissioning editor with a publishing company. As such it was her job to recommend acceptance or rejection of manuscripts submitted by new authors, to chase after established authors and persuade them to write books for her company, and to dream up her own writing projects and then find authors able and willing to carry them out. 'It was a heavenly job, exactly what I wanted to do in life. I travelled around a lot, I met interesting people, I worked with books, and people respected my abilities. I think, in the end, I was better at my job than Tom is at his. I know I enjoyed it more.' When the first child arrived, Julia took maternity leave and then went back to work, leaving the baby with a baby-minder. But, 'When I was at work I couldn't concentrate as I used to. My heart wasn't in it in the same way. I kept thinking of the baby and telling myself what a rotten mother I was to leave her like that. And I worried that she would become more attached to the baby-minder than to me. I felt guilty and jealous by turns, and in the end I decided I had to give up the job and be at home full time.'

Julia told herself she would return to work in the near future, but she and Tom wanted more than one child, and felt that the best way was to have them close together. So Julia's dream of returning to work receded further and further into the future. Looked at realistically, she also had to tell herself that a career as a commissioning editor, with its travelling and its irregular hours, was in any case incompatible with bringing up three small children. So now she doesn't know what to do. Well-qualified, with a good university degree behind her and a good track record in publishing, she sees little chance of ever being able to find a job which will suit her interests and abilities.

'By the time the children are big enough for me to fit in a career, I'll probably be too old and too mentally rusty to be any use. After all, if I can't go back to publishing I'll have to start something else from scratch. And I always wanted to work in publishing, from as early as I can remember. I'm starting to get into such a state that not only can I never relax during the day, I wake every night with feelings of sheer panic. I lie there sweating away and with my heart thumping, and feel so desperate sometimes it's as much as I can do not to run over to the window and jump out.'

Julia's problem is shared by many other women, and as with most of the case studies in this book, I return to it in a later chapter to discuss the solution.

Julia illustrates the fact that for many women, the very years that they need to spend building their careers are the very years when their children need them most. To add to Julia's frustration, she thinks Tom is unable to understand what is worrying her. A considerate husband in one way, he doesn't want Julia ever to feel she has to go back to work in order to balance the household budget. It is his job, he feels, to earn enough money to keep them all. But what he fails to appreciate is the unfulfilled side of Julia, the loss of identity, the feeling of stagnation, of the years passing, of wasted abilities, of missed opportunities, of boredom and under-extension. He fails to recognize how much publishing means to her, and how good she is at it. Nor does he provide her with the help in the house and with the children that would give her a little of the space she needs. Without being too chauvinistic, he nevertheless sees the home and the family as her side of the bargain, while his side is to submit to the discipline of work and see to it that he can provide properly for everyone's material needs.

One of the worrying features about a case like Julia's is what will happen when the children finally do grow up and need her less? At the moment, much as she enjoys them, she finds herself looking forward to this time, even though it may come too late for her to pick up her career where she left off. But so much of her identity is now bound up with being a mother, and with the feeling of sacrifice associated with it, that when the children no longer need her to the same extent in this role, there is the fear that, like a redundant worker, she will have precious little left of herself. The result is that she may try to hang on to her children for too long, or expect 'gratitude' from them for the sacrifices she has made on their behalf, or may quite simply find herself aimless and depressed, no longer knowing what her role in life is.

'If I could only get away on my own for a few days,' Julia complains, 'that would help me to think properly about myself, and to sort myself out. But it's so hard to get away. And even if I did, I think I'd be worrying about the family and about whether they were all right. I'd be imagining all sorts of things going wrong. As it is I find I always seem to be terrified that something awful is going to happen to the children or to Tom, and that it'll be my fault for not loving them enough. I know it's all so stupid, but I just can't seem to help myself.'

Interestingly, when I talked to Tom, he also referred to getting away from home, which he does from time to time on business trips, and confessed that on the occasions he manages to do so he feels a heady sense of freedom. 'It takes me by surprise. I may be on the plane or in my first night in the hotel, and suddenly, without thinking about it, I feel a lightness, a sort of liberation. As if I'm rediscovering something in myself. A sort of uplift at being away from the family and able to stop seeing myself as father and husband and householder and breadwinner. Don't get me wrong. I wouldn't want to be away for too long. But I do feel I expand when I have some time to myself, like filling a blank part of the canvas.'

On questioning, Tom admits he doesn't worry about the family when he's away. 'Julia is so efficient. She has everything tied up. I know she can look after herself and the children. It's no problem for me to be away.'

OWNING YOUR OWN LIFE

Julia's problem results from several things: the loss of her job and of the interest and involvement that went with it, the loss of future career prospects, the feeling she is trapped within the house and the family, the worry that her best years are passing by, the inability of her husband fully to understand her position. What these add up to is the fact that Julia does not own her own life. Her life script is still being written for her rather than by her, and there's no immediate sign that things are going to change. In many ways it looks as if she has less personal power – power over her own life and what she does with it – than she had during her childhood and adolescent years.

Julia's problems appear to be all *out there*, in other words, circumstantial facts not of her own making. But even Julia has none of the buttons to press that I talked about on page 28. She certainly needs to change some of what is happening *out there*, but she mustn't ignore the fact that everything she feels, from the anxiety about her family to her feelings of panic in the middle of the night, are something she does to herself. There are no magic buttons, remember.

What can Julia do? What can anyone do who feels a worrying lack of power over their life script, and wants to change it?

For Julia and for anyone else who wants to work on a psychological problem, whether it is mild or serious, the place to start is to take over the writing of key parts of your life script. The ground has already been prepared by the five steps we've already looked at:

Step 1: recognize the extent of the hold your thoughts and emotions have over you

Step 2: find out more about your own thought and emotional processes so that you can bring them more under the control of your conscious will

Step 3: stop blaming yourself for the fact that up to now you're not more in charge of your inner life

Step 4: recognize that the possession of psychological problems isn't a sign of weakness.

Step 5: acknowledge that you do have the power to change things, that it is possible for you to be much more fully in charge of your inner life.

These steps are, if you like, the preparations you make before setting out on a voyage, in this case a voyage of transformation within yourself. You're now ready to take the next five steps, which are the journey proper. It begins with Step 6:

Step 6: find where you are now.

Step 6 is the subject of the next chapter.

5

WHERE ARE YOU NOW?

Finding where you are now is a priority on any journey. If you want to take a journey, even if you aren't yet sure of your destination, you need to know exactly where you're starting from. It's no good imagining you're starting from London when in fact you live in Edinburgh. The timetable of trains from London won't be much use to you, and until you realize your mistake you'll spend a long time standing on the platform waiting for a train that never comes.

Step 6, 'Find where you are now', is a step towards self-understanding, and provides you with details about yourself that enable you to identify more clearly what it is about your life that you want to change, and why. It enables you to take a long look at yourself, not only to recognize your shortcomings, but also to identify where you may be judging yourself too harshly.

DRAWING A SELF-PORTRAIT

There are a number of ways in which you can start this self-exploration. The following method is one that works best for many people.

▶ Exercise 9: Starting your self-exploration

Below is a list of describing words and their opposites. Look at each pair of describing words in turn, and put a tick in *one* of the five boxes separating them. If you feel that the word in the left-hand column describes you best, put your tick in the box immediately next to it. If you feel the word in the right-hand column is the most appropriate, put your tick next to that instead. The three boxes in the middle represent gradations between these two extremes. If the extremes aren't right for you, use whichever of these inner boxes is more appropriate. The very middle box represents the neutral point.

There are no right and wrong answers, although obviously some of the words look more flattering than others. Avoid trying to give a good impression of yourself just for the sake of it. The only person you will be misleading is yourself. No-one need see the list after you have completed it unless you want them to. The list is a long one. Take your time over it, but don't agonize too much over each pair of words. Often your first reaction is the most accurate one.

It's best to make a list of the words on a separate sheet of paper and use this for your ticks. The act of writing down the words helps you reflect on their meaning, and also means you don't have to mark the book.

quick	□	□	□	□	□	slow
dull	□	□	□	□	□	clever
boring	□	□	□	□	□	interesting
free	□	□	□	□	□	captive
low-spirited	□	□	□	□	□	high-spirited
happy	□	□	□	□	□	sad
fulfilled	□	□	□	□	□	unfulfilled
pessimistic	□	□	□	□	□	optimistic
friendly	□	□	□	□	□	unfriendly
active	□	□	□	□	□	passive

assertive	☐	☐	☐	☐	☐	unassertive
backward-looking	☐	☐	☐	☐	☐	forward-looking
discontented	☐	☐	☐	☐	☐	contented
gentle	☐	☐	☐	☐	☐	stern
humorous	☐	☐	☐	☐	☐	sober
unpopular	☐	☐	☐	☐	☐	popular
tough-minded	☐	☐	☐	☐	☐	tender-minded
introverted	☐	☐	☐	☐	☐	extroverted
ungrateful	☐	☐	☐	☐	☐	grateful
loved	☐	☐	☐	☐	☐	unloved
kind	☐	☐	☐	☐	☐	unkind
tough-minded	☐	☐	☐	☐	☐	tender-minded
inhibited	☐	☐	☐	☐	☐	uninhibited
successful	☐	☐	☐	☐	☐	unsuccessful
fearful (mostly)	☐	☐	☐	☐	☐	fearless (mostly)
quiet	☐	☐	☐	☐	☐	talkative
ambitious	☐	☐	☐	☐	☐	unambitious
inconsiderate	☐	☐	☐	☐	☐	considerate
indecisive	☐	☐	☐	☐	☐	decisive
organized	☐	☐	☐	☐	☐	disorganized
outspoken	☐	☐	☐	☐	☐	reticent

lazy	☐	☐	☐	☐	☐	hard-working
flexible	☐	☐	☐	☐	☐	inflexible
courageous	☐	☐	☐	☐	☐	timid
aggressive	☐	☐	☐	☐	☐	peaceful
secretive	☐	☐	☐	☐	☐	open
vulnerable	☐	☐	☐	☐	☐	safe
nice (mostly)	☐	☐	☐	☐	☐	nasty (mostly)
tense	☐	☐	☐	☐	☐	relaxed
insecure	☐	☐	☐	☐	☐	secure
patient	☐	☐	☐	☐	☐	impatient
soft	☐	☐	☐	☐	☐	hard
unloving	☐	☐	☐	☐	☐	loving
forgiving	☐	☐	☐	☐	☐	unforgiving
responsible	☐	☐	☐	☐	☐	irresponsible
unreliable	☐	☐	☐	☐	☐	reliable
formal	☐	☐	☐	☐	☐	informal
conscientious	☐	☐	☐	☐	☐	unconscientious
depressed	☐	☐	☐	☐	☐	undepressed
tidy	☐	☐	☐	☐	☐	untidy
warm	☐	☐	☐	☐	☐	cold
creative	☐	☐	☐	☐	☐	uncreative
quick-tempered	☐	☐	☐	☐	☐	even-tempered

vague	☐	☐	☐	☐	☐	precise
decisive	☐	☐	☐	☐	☐	indecisive
detached	☐	☐	☐	☐	☐	involved
trusting	☐	☐	☐	☐	☐	suspicious
reserved	☐	☐	☐	☐	☐	outgoing

When you've worked through the list, what do you deduce about yourself from the ticks you've made? They provide a pattern, a profile of certain relevant aspects of yourself. They give you an idea of where you are now, which should help you to think a little more clearly about yourself and about the things you want to change.

Now give a copy of the list to someone who knows you well, without letting them see your ticks, and ask them to fill it in to reflect what they think about you. Tell them under no circumstances to try to be kind to you. You are interested only in their honest opinion. Anything else will not only be useless to you, it will actively hinder you in your progress towards self-understanding.

Compare the two lists, in private if you prefer. Is there a close measure of agreement? If not, look at the discrepancies between your ratings and theirs. Does the other person tend to mark you in a more positive and favourable way than you do, or is it the other way around? If there are major differences between the two sets of ratings, it's advisable to get someone else (more than one person if you can) to give you their ratings as well. Don't let them see either your own version or the one already produced for you before they've carried out the exercise. You want their own unbiased opinion.

If you still find a big discrepancy between what you think about yourself and what other people think, there's a good chance you are marking yourself too leniently or too strictly. This is an important finding, because it means that in life generally you may be judging yourself in the wrong way. It's a point to which we will return in due course.

Now look back at your self-rating. If it agrees fairly well with those of other people, there's a good chance that it's an accurate enough picture of the way you are now. Add to your list any other pairs of describing words that you think are relevant, and again tick one of the five boxes on the scale. Look at these additions and see what more they tell you about yourself.

Think also about your physical appearance. Nothing relating specifically to this appears on the list. We're not interested in whether you're stunningly handsome or beautiful (very few of us think we are), but whether you feel comfortable with yourself. Can you look in the mirror without always wishing some feature were different? Or without always making minor repairs and adjustments – tidying (or ruffling artistically) a lock of hair, powdering the nose (women), straightening the tie (men) and so on? Small as these gestures are, their frequent and unnecessary repetition suggests not just an over-preoccupation with the appearance but an insecurity about it, which can contribute to a general lack of confidence in yourself.

Do you look and feel reasonably physically balanced and co-ordinated? The body and the face reflect how we feel about ourselves. Some psychologists even use the term 'body armour' to describe the tense, unnatural way in which many of us hold ourselves, as if our bodies are braced to receive the emotional blows that fell upon us in the early years of our life script and after. (Thus hunched shoulders may be a sign of defeat and depression, a rigid back a sign of inflexibility, a furrowed brow a sign of anxiety.)

Finally, go back to the list and underline six words which seem best to sum you up. Write a few sentences describing yourself in the third person to an imaginary person who has never met you, using these six key words. You can add in other descriptive words from the list too if you like, but make sure that these six words are the main focus. Look carefully at this written description of yourself. It's a self-portrait of the person you think you are.

When you feel this self-portrait is as accurate as you can make it, do as you did with the list of describing words. Give it to someone who knows you well and whom you trust, and ask them whether they think it sums you up. Listen carefully to what they say, in particular to any points where they disagree with what you've written. Don't try and convince them they're wrong. Rightly or wrongly, this is the impression they have of you, and it tells you important things about the way in which you come across to others.

Your Relationship with Your Parents

Your relationship with your family involves issues that are too extensive to have been included in Exercise 8, and need to be dealt with separately now.

Assuming one or both of your parents are still alive, how influential do they remain in writing your life script? One of the best ways to answer this question is to examine key issues in your relationships with them. It's helpful to score each of these on a 5-point scale from 5 (very good) through good (4), mediocre (3), poor (2) down to 1 (very poor). If both parents are alive and you feel you differ significantly in your relationship with each of them, consider each parent separately. The same issues may apply equally to parents-in-law.

These are the key issues:

Openness. Complete openness means that you can be honest and direct with your parents about all aspects of your life, including your innermost feelings. It also means you can criticise them, disagree with them, and refuse to accept advice or help without their taking offence.

The ability to feel you can be open with those close to you is an excellent indication of the degree of security you enjoy in a relationship. If you can't be honest with your parents about yourself and your attitudes and feelings, there's some uncertainty in your relationship with them. You're afraid that if they know what you really think they will disapprove of you as a person, perhaps even withdraw some of their love from you. Deep down, you still feel they don't accept you for being who you are, but for being who they think you are.

Acceptance. This issue was dealt with at some length in Chapter 1. But parental acceptance – or rather the lack of it – still lies at the heart of many psychological problems even for adults. Parental approval still provides the yardstick against which they measure themselves and their achievements. Many people still feel they have to prove themselves to an ambitious father or mother, or (particularly in the case of the woman-mother relationship) to handle their *emotional* life in a way parents will approve of. Some parents have an idealized picture of what their children should be 'like' even when they're grown up. It might be a father who has an idealized picture of womanhood to which he expects his daughter to conform, or a mother who has an idealized picture of manhood which she expects to be realized in her son.

Understanding. Acceptance and understanding aren't quite the same thing. Your parents may happily accept you, may love, admire and respect you, yet you may feel that they don't understand you, that there is a sense in which they don't properly know you, either because they never have done, or because over the years you've grown apart. Individuals who don't feel properly understood in this way often confess that the understanding they want from their parents has nothing to do with indulgence or tolerance, but comes through someone knowing what we're doing and liking our reasons for doing it. Lack of this understanding can leave us conscious of a need to justify ourselves, even to switch – in our careers, in our personal lives – to things our parents *will* understand.

Space. Space means that you feel your parents don't try to meddle too much in your life, to control what you do and what you think, to interfere in your career or in your domestic or financial affairs or in your relationship with your partner or with your children. Space means that they allow you to be yourself. Space means that you feel your parents are not trying to live your life for you, or – just as vital – trying to live their lives through you.

Equality. In a good relationship, there is usually a sense of equality, of partnership, rather than a sense that one party is always dominated by the other. Although parents are the senior partners in the early chapters of your life script, did they progressively relinquish this position as you grew older? If equality operates, you should now feel that your relationship with them is one of virtual equals, with both them and you respectful of the position and of the rights and status of the other.

Support. Support means the confidence that your parents, without denying you your space, will give you appropriate help when you need it. And give it without unnecessary lecturing or conditions.

Freedom from guilt. Of all emotions, guilt is one of the most destructive. It means a constant self-punishment that can destroy our confidence and belief in ourselves, and even result in self-rejection and self-dislike. It stems from a continuing sense of wronging or of having wronged others. Many of us carry a heavy burden of it from our childhood, when we were especially vulnerable to the disapproval of others. I am sometimes told by clients of all ages that they cannot be in the parental home for ten minutes, or even speak to a parent on the telephone, without being made to feel guilty for something they have said or done or not said or not done, or for some unacceptable motive or feeling that the parent concerned *imagines* they are harbouring towards him or her.

Love. 'I know my mother/father loves me, but they've never ever said so,' is a frequent complaint of clients. I talked in Chapter 3 about the importance of demonstrating affection if people are to be helped towards self-acceptance and the self-confidence that goes with it. Of course there is more to love than loving words and the occasional hug. But direct expressions of love are very important. Denied these in childhood, many adults find it has left them wounded in their ability to give and receive love, and with a deep sense of something missing from their lives.

Health and strength. We're naturally concerned for the mental and physical health of our parents. But an ailing parent who needs special attention does place a burden on a son or daughter, no matter how willingly we may accept it. The burden is lessened if the parent doesn't over-control, and leaves some of the decisions on what care is needed to us. The ability to have a say in decision-making is an important one if we're in the position of carer, since it helps us retain some autonomy over our life script, particularly vital at a time when our room for manoeuvre may be very limited.

Enjoyment. Most people go through the experience of not 'enjoying' their parents very much during the adolescent years. In an otherwise good parent-child relationship, this is simply a stage in our adjustment into adulthood, and into the changes this brings about in the way we see life. In adolescence, parents are usually no longer the providers of treats, of excitement, of fun generally. These things now come more from the peer group, and it is the company of the peer group that we usually seek. But once into adult life, the relationship with parents should enter into a new phase that brings the enjoyment of shared interests and mature companionship.

People sometimes complain that, much as they love their parents, this companionship is marred by the fact that they still feel talked down to by their parents, or that their parents simply talk too much, assaulting them with minor details about life that mean little to them, and turning each meeting into an ordeal that leaves them feeling bad for not listening properly.

FRANCESCA: A DESTRUCTIVE PARENTAL RELATIONSHIP
The following is an example of the extent to which relationships with parents can still write our life script for us well into adult life.

Francesca and Brian have recently separated, and Francesca insists the fault lies with Brian's mother, Monica. From the day they first met, Francesca felt uneasy with Monica, and although Monica seemed in favour of the marriage, Francesca felt there was something odd about her whole attitude which should have made her sense trouble ahead. After the marriage, Monica sold her house and bought another one almost opposite the newly-weds. Much too big for her needs, the house was in an advanced state of disrepair, and Monica began to make increasing demands upon Brian's time and energies in order to help her put it to rights. 'He was over there most evenings and weekends, and never seemed to have any space for me,' says Francesca.

Worse still, Monica demanded a key to Francesca and Brian's house, and would let herself in during the day, when Francesca and Brian were both out at work. Francesca would frequently come home to find the house rearranged 'in the way', Monica would claim, 'Brian likes best'. When Francesca demanded he put a stop to this interference, Brian hedged, avoiding the issue and claiming things would 'settle down' when Monica was properly ensconced in her own house.

'But they didn't,' says Francesca. 'They got worse. And when in the end I felt I had to have it out with Monica, she flew into a rage and accused me of selfishness, and of not loving Brian properly. When I told Brian, he had a go at me too, and told me I'd no business to go upsetting his mother like that. He didn't seem to care how upset I was.'

Things deteriorated even further. Monica insisted on coming on holiday with Brian and Francesca, 'and ruined things for me by disagreeing with everything I said, and by smiling knowingly at Brian each time she did, as if to say, 'I told you so; now see what kind of woman you've married.' She ruined Christmas for us in the same way, criticizing all my efforts to please her. She wouldn't allow us to go anywhere without taking her with us. She made me feel inadequate and hopeless at every turn, and although I was furious with myself for it, I ended up feeling guilty about her, and even guilty about Brian, as if Monica was right and I was a rotten wife.'

The worst part about it was that Brian refused point-blank to confront his mother. 'He seemed to be on her side,' says Francesca. 'I think he was frightened of her. If she spoke sharply to him about anything, he would be depressed for days. I felt we were drifting apart, but there was nothing I could do about it. He wouldn't discuss his mother with me, and after a time I noticed he was criticizing me for the same things and in the same way that Monica was.'

The last straw came when Francesca lost her temper with Monica one night after some particularly wounding criticism, and ordered her out of the house. Monica refused to go, and announced she'd only 'let' Francesca marry her son because she thought she would make a dutiful wife and daughter-in-law. 'Now you've proved you're neither of these things, it's you who should leave, not me.' Francesca appealed to Brian for support, but he again took his mother's part, and blamed Francesca for starting the scene. In a very emotional state by this time, Francesca demanded that Brian choose between her and his mother. Brian refused, and the next day Francesca packed her bags and walked out.

Francesca was justified in thinking that although she was the one who suffered most from Monica's behaviour, it was really Brian who had the problems. In effect he was still a small boy, dependent upon his mother for direction on how he should and should not live his life, and for his good opinion of himself. Until Brian was able to break free, there was clearly no future for Francesca in a relationship with him.

Learning from These Issues

Once you have been through the above list of important issues in your relationships with your parents and have scored it from your point of view, what can be learnt from the exercise? We can't be dogmatic and say that a score of so many points means your parents are no longer controlling your life script, while a lower score is an indication that they are. The issues are too complex for that. But clearly a run of low scores, or even low scores on particular issues, shows that problems exist. It is for you to decide from these scores where action needs to be taken.

For example, you may feel that low scores indicate the need to speak out in the areas where your parents fail to accept you or where you end up feeling guilty. Speaking out on these or on other issues which we've just been looking at is never easy, especially as you will have a natural reluctance to hurt or offend your parents. But there is a very helpful rule to remember here. When speaking out, *direct criticism of your parents* may not be appropriate, but you do have a perfect right to *refer to your own feelings.*

Thus instead of accusing your parents of their shortcomings in not accepting you or in trying to make you feel guilty, you can inform them, simply and directly, that this lack of acceptance troubles you, or that your fear of guilt leads you to feel anxious when you meet them. If we attempt always to protect parents from knowing how we feel, then we are denying them the chance to know us better, just as in other ways they may be denying us the chance to be open with them.

In Francesca's case, it is possible that Brian's weakness would have made it very difficult for her to save her marriage, whatever she did. But when reflecting on her behaviour, she admitted afterwards that she had never told Monica how her interference in the marriage made her feel. Instead, she had chosen to tell Brian, who clearly did not have the strength or the courage to talk to Monica on her behalf. And when she finally tried to order Monica out of the house, she made the mistake of confronting hers with her own conduct rather than explaining these feelings. Monica was clearly in the wrong, but confronting her didn't help. It was just possible that, bound up as she was in herself and in her relationship with her son, she had no idea of how badly Francesca was feeling.

But whatever situation demands a decision, you are the person best placed to take it, since only you know all the relevant circumstances. There may for instance be issues on which your parents have a great deal of influence over your life script but where you feel things should remain as they are. You may feel that although your parents' interference with some aspects of your life is irksome at times, it is nevertheless still necessary to you. Their control over your financial decisions, for example, may be important if you're no good with money. Their control over your children may be welcome if you are limited in what you can do for them yourself. Their control over your career may be helpful if you tend to be a little impulsive or lacking in direction.

As in so many areas of human psychology, one can't generalize too much about the right or wrong answers on any of these issues. Part of the process of psychological growth involves reaching the point where *you* feel able to identify the things that most affect your life and to reach mature and properly informed decisions about them.

Your Relationship with Your Partner

By partner I mean husband or wife or the person with whom you have a stable live-in relationship, but the term can also apply to boyfriend or girlfriend where the relationship is a close one, and where this relationship significantly influences your life and the way in which you see yourself. (If you're not in this situation at the moment, you can skip this section if you like.)

You can apply the issues dealt with in the context of your parents to your relationship with a partner, but we need to add further points in connection with some of them, and one or two new issues.

Acceptance and understanding. If our life script isn't to be taken over in the wrong way by our partner, then in addition to their love and support we need a degree of acceptance and understanding. Of all relationships, few are more rewarding than the one where the partner accepts and understands us for what we are, and doesn't try to change us into the person they think we should be. As I stressed earlier, there's always the need to compromise in a relationship and give up something of ourselves to the other person, but if we are forced to surrender things central to who we are, or to sacrifice openness in order to play-act the person our partner wants us to be, then our life script is no longer in our own hands.

Unqualified acceptance by a partner of the person we really are, rather than of some unrealistic image they have of us, is one of the most important aids to psychological health adult life can bring. It is said that 'no man is a failure until his wife thinks he is', and the saying works equally well the other way around. As long as there is one person in the world who loves and accepts us, then we are helped to go on loving and accepting ourselves.

Shared interests. The existence of shared interests (perhaps in hobbies and leisure interests, perhaps in occupations,

WHERE ARE YOU NOW?

perhaps in sport, perhaps in religious or political activities) is another important factor in a relationship. Shared interests bring people closer and mean they don't feel excluded from each other's enthusiasms. They also mean there are more aspects of our partner to which we can relate. Shared interests to which both partners contribute their fair share can also help lead to equality in a relationship. But no matter how they are shared, these interests broaden the horizons of a partnership and give people more opportunity to do things together.

Equality and space. Equality depends also upon sharing responsibilities, so that both you and your partner are involved in decision-making. Complete equality is of course rarely achieved, and some people in any case prefer their partner to take the leading role. But a degree of equality arises naturally in any relationship where each partner respects the other enough to want them to be a rounded person in their own right. The same is true of space. Space means allowing the partner to go on functioning as a unique individual as well as being a member of the partnership. It means the freedom to pursue separate interests as well as shared ones, and the freedom to have some privacy and time to oneself when needed.

Equality and space within a relationship also help keep each partner feeling significant and personally powerful. In a relationship, it's good to know we've a right to go on developing as individuals, and that our partner cares about this development on our behalf and is prepared to give us the scope we need.

Health and strength. These may seem less appropriate when talking about a partner than when talking about parents. But even without the presence of physical illness, one partner in a relationship may lack the physical drive and energy of the other, and thus restrict the things that can be done together. It's nice to know that when we want to redecorate the living room, our partner is keen to make the effort too. Or that when he or she wants to go out in the evening, we don't prefer falling asleep in front of the television. Or that when one of us wants to climb a mountain at the weekend, to go for long walks, to take holidays in distant countries, to dig the garden, to support good causes, to take part in whatever is going on, the other has the enthusiasm to come along too. Compatibility of physical energy is often overlooked when relationships are discussed, but it plays an important part in keeping things harmonious and well balanced.

The same is true for psychological energy. It's good when partners have compatible mental abilities, with each able to hold their own in the discussions and inevitable disputes that arise between two people living together. It's even better when their personalities are compatible. This avoids the kind of issues that can arise when, for example, one partner is extroverted by temperament and orientated towards social experience and plenty of external stimulation and excitement, while the other is introverted and orientated towards inner states of mind and quieter and less socially-demanding pursuits.

Of course, compatibility doesn't mean we must have an identical personality to our partner. Sometimes differences in personality can complement each other, as when one of us provides a calming influence upon the other, or when one of us socially stimulates or amuses or inspires the other. The important thing is that we feel we are generally pulling in the same direction as our partner, and not placing too many restrictions upon the life scripts they want to write for themselves.

Sexual compatibility. The sex drive is a natural and powerful instinct in both men and women. The human race would not have survived without it. The sex act is a joyful and life-enhancing experience, and there is evidence that people who have an open attitude towards it, not clouded by guilt or prudery or distaste, are psychologically healthier and happier than those who do not.

But by the very nature of its power, the sex drive can lead to difficulties. If one partner's sex drive is by nature much stronger than that of the other, or if one partner suffers from sexual inhibitions, or if one partner is initially concerned only with personal rather than mutual satisfaction, then re-adjustment is called for. Provided both partners recognize the need, this comes about through mutual understanding and patience. The need for these qualities extends to the amount of physical affection partners give to and receive from each other, and to their attitudes towards sexual experiences outside the partnership.

All the issues listed above are part of the *shared environment* of a relationship, which also includes the home and the way each partner thinks it should be run, the neighbours and each partner's attitude towards them, and financial matters and the domestic budget. In each of these areas, mutual re-adjustment and learning may be necessary. Nowhere is this more obvious than where children are involved.

BILL: TROUBLE WITH A TEENAGER

When Bill consulted me about problems with his teenage daughter, he revealed that what worried him most was the fact that disagreements with his wife Susan over how best to handle these problems were even beginning to threaten his marriage. He instanced particularly the case of his daughter's bedroom, which was like an obstacle course of discarded clothes, books, papers, school work, sports equipment and a host of less easily identified items. Bill felt this showed a complete disregard for the home he had worked so hard to provide for his family. Yet for Susan, their daughter's behaviour was simply that of a typical teenager. Anyway, she argued, a teenage girl had a right to her own space if her home really was to be her home. Bill was genuinely perplexed at the arguments this led to between Susan and himself and at the way in which his daughter's behaviour appeared so comprehensively to have taken over the script of their twenty-year marriage. Clearly, Bill and Susan had a great deal of talking to do if they were to agree on how to relate to their daughter, and begin to take the management of their script back into their own hands.

TANIA: UNFAIR DIVISION OF LABOUR

A very different example of the power of children to influence the life script of a marriage was provided by

Tania and her husband Michael. Tania and Michael had a toddler of two years and an older child of four. The problem in their case was that Tania felt everything to do with the children was left to her. Michael not only did nothing to help with their physical care, he also left all matters of discipline to Tania. She was the one who fed, washed and dressed the children and got up to them in the night, and she was also the one who had to deal with their tantrums, jealousies and squabbles.

The result was that Tania felt increasingly exploited, and increasingly irritated and disenchanted with Michael. She saw him as failing in his duties as father, and confessed to the secret fear that if he continued to leave the disciplining to her the children would come to prefer Michael as they grew older. Tania's case is typical of the situation in which many young mothers find themselves, and we shall return to it in Chapter 8.

Some Dos and Don'ts

In carrying out the exercises in this chapter to help you discover where you are now, there are certain important points to keep in mind.

1. You don't have to share your discovery of where you are now with anyone else unless you want to. If you feel uneasy at the thought of sharing, keep your discovery to yourself for now. You will probably feel like sharing later, when you are more in control of your life.

2. Since you don't have to share, be completely open with yourself.

3. If it's hard to be open because you don't want to face some of the things you're finding out about yourself and about your life, relax. You're in good company. Most people feel the same way as you. But the very fact that it *is* hard shows the power the early chapters of your life script still have over you. It's because other people didn't accept you for what you are during the

writing of these chapters that you still find it difficult to accept yourself. Part of the healing process is to begin this acceptance by being honest with yourself now. Don't be daunted if in the process you discover a number of major areas of your life where things seem to be unsatisfactory and change looks necessary. A step-by-step approach to these problem areas, in the way outlined in the next chapters, allows you to keep them in perspective, and to identify the ways in which they can best be managed.

4. Write down or draw the discovery you are making about where you are now (see Exercise 9). The act of writing or of drawing not only gives you a record to which you can return and ponder over later, it also – like any creative activity – helps you to get in touch with your unconscious and recover from its vast treasure chest more and more memories relating back to the early chapters of your script, and more and more pieces of helpful self-knowledge.

The work you do on your life script should never involve unconscious flights into fantasy. The main aim of Step 6 is to find a realistic answer to the question 'where am I at this moment in my life?'. By now, you have lots of information to help you supply this answer. The next exercise will enable you to complete this answer and put you in a position to decide in the steps that follow how and in what way you want to begin the process of change.

▶ Exercise 10: Your professional, personal and leisure lives

Write down three headings: 'My Professional Life', 'My Personal Life', and 'My Leisure Life'. Under each heading draw two columns and label them *Out there* and *In here* respectively. Under each of the three headings write down how your life appears to you *out there* and *in here* in the light of the discoveries you have now made about yourself. If you're at home full-time caring for the family, enter this under the 'Professional Life' column. Remember point 2 on page 100 and be as open with yourself as you can. If you find there is a lot of resistance inside you to being open, write down as much as you can about this resistance. What form does it take? How does it feel? Now try and identify why it's there. What is it you are resisting, and why are you resisting it? If you can't come up with satisfactory answers, note this down and resolve to return to the matter from time to time until you can.

Your entries under each of the three headings can be as long or as short as you like. Neither length nor brevity are necessarily right or wrong in work of this kind. The most important thing is that you feel you have written what it is necessary to write. Notice if there are major differences between what you're writing under the *Out There* column and what you're writing under *In Here*. For example, your professional life may look very successful *Out There*. You may have achieved the promotion you wanted, and you may be making a very good living. But *In Here* you may feel bored and unfulfilled in your work. You may consider you're full of unrealized potential. You may find your colleagues uncongenial, your working environment unattractive, and your standards and beliefs under attack. Wide discrepancies of this kind indicate to you that when you come in due course to write your conclusions to this exercise, you will be much clearer as to the way you really feel about your life.

If you find it difficult to write something under any or all of the three headings in this exercise, draw pictures instead. They can be representational or symbolic, the choice is yours. But don't become so carried away with perfecting the artwork that you forget its purpose. What matters is not pretty pictures but pictures that say something about yourself. You can combine writing and pictures if you wish.

At the end of the exercise, put down the heading *Conclusions* and write or draw what the exercise has told you.

JENNIFER: HEMMED IN BY 'ME'

Let's look at how one person carried out Exercise 10 (see page 104). Jennifer is thirty-eight, married, but now separated from her husband for three years. She has remained friendly with him, and he has several times asked her to go back. She now finds herself wondering whether to do so or to break away altogether and start proceedings for divorce. She currently works as a medical secretary in a large teaching hospital, and in the descriptive writing at the end of Exercise 9 (page 83) she describes herself as a creative, over-emotional, extroverted person who is warm, trusting and loving. She is, however, subject to periods of depression which she hides from the rest of the world under a determinedly cheerful manner, but which lately have made her feel increasingly as if she is 'hemmed in by *me*'. She thinks it is her extroversion that makes it, for example, hard for her to function properly at work if her office door is closed. It gives her a sense of being 'isolated and a bit unreal', and she has taken to propping it permanently open.

Jennifer added the following conclusion at the end of Exercise 10.

Conclusions. I'm sure there are lots of things in me that I can't face. I haven't faced the reasons why my marriage failed. I haven't faced what stopped me trying to take up a creative career when I left school instead of doing a secretarial course. I haven't faced what is happening to me now, and why I get depressed and feel panicky and hemmed in by me. I think some of it has to do with being the youngest of four children, and the only girl. Someone else was always there to take decisions for me. When I grew older, I didn't feel able to take decisions for myself about what to do with my life. I didn't even know what decisions I ought to be taking for myself, and what decisions I ought to let others take for me.

I think some of it has to do with being afraid. Afraid of taking responsibility or of taking risks. Afraid of committing myself to the wrong things when there's no-one there to help me escape from them. Afraid of

Professional Life

Out There
Successful. I seem to have got more or less where I wanted to be. I'm popular with colleagues, and people think I do a good job.

In Here
Lately I've been feeling very restless. I can't see myself being a medical secretary for the rest of my life. Don't know what else I could do. I've started dreaming of being an artist, but I haven't the talent.

Personal Life

Out There
No obvious shortage of friends, though I invite people to my place more often than I get asked back. I'm physically quite attractive and have had two affairs since leaving my husband, neither of them very serious. People see me as happy to be uncommitted. I'm well-dressed and always immaculate, but somehow artificial. I look artificial.

In Here
Lonely, and rather scared. I'm 38 and my chances of having children are rapidly receding. I don't know whether I want them, but I'd like the option. I've started getting panicky when alone, or when I think too much about the future. My marriage wasn't working and I don't want to go back, but unless I can handle this loneliness I may have to.

Leisure Life

Out There
I play badminton and tennis. I swim twice a week, enjoy music and the theatre, and take two holidays abroad each year with girl friends.

In Here
I enjoy all these things, but not as much as I would like. I feel as if I'm waiting for something to happen but I don't know what. Whatever it is, I feel I'm powerless to bring it about for myself.

going too deeply into myself in case I find all sorts of bad bits which will make me hate who I am. I haven't faced why I can't decide even whether I'd really like children or not. But a thought does keep coming up. I've tried to push it away, but it's still there, and now I've started this work on myself it's beginning to interest me. It's the thought that my failed marriage and the fact that my two affairs never looked like becoming serious – *and* my inability to decide whether I want children or not – may mean I don't really know how to love. What a strange thing to say about yourself when you're thirty-eight! We all take it for granted that we know how to love. But do we? What is love? Is it something I should have learnt? Or was I born knowing it? If I've missed out, why have I missed out? If I can't love others, is it possible for them to love me?

The more Jennifer thought about the results of the exercise, the more she came to understand why it was she felt hemmed in by herself. Because she was so afraid of making real decisions about her life, part of her had become rigid and over-controlled, afraid to let the other more spontaneous side of her think for itself in case it decided to go off and do something she couldn't handle. She drew a picture showing a woman 'dressed to kill' (the term was hers) glaring menacingly at another woman naked except for ribbons trailing from her long flowing hair. When asked to add her name to the picture, she placed it exactly between the two women.

CREATIVITY AND YOU

Like many people, both those who call themselves creative and those who don't, Jennifer found that drawing a picture was a very helpful way of clarifying how she felt about herself and her life. Why should this be?

As I discuss more fully in Chapter 8, words are very powerful things. We live most of our days in a highly verbal environment, and most of our communication with ourselves and with others is through the form of words. For all their many advantages, words can have a very controlling influence upon our self-expression. Most of the prohibitions contained in our life script are to do with words. 'Don't do this', 'Don't do that', 'Don't make a scene', 'Don't shout', 'Don't cry/rage/love/touch/laugh' or do many of the other things that express our emotional life. In time some of these prohibitions go deep into our unconscious (are *internalized*) and act to repress the spontaneous, creative side of ourselves that helps us keep in touch with our deeper wishes, wants and feelings.

Drawing or painting a picture can often help to bypass these internal controls. Provided, that is, we discard the idea we must produce a 'good' or 'realistic' or 'nice' work of art. The only approach that counts is to pick up pencil or brush and put down on paper whatever comes. Don't allow words to intrude between your creativity and the paper. And don't allow words to evaluate what you're doing or discourage you from doing it. When you've finished, look at the results, whether representational or abstract, and see what they tell you.

If you find it hard to overcome a dislike for painting or drawing but still want a method to help you unlock your creativity, you can stay with words, but try using them in a different way. Try writing a simple little story, in which one of the characters stands for yourself. Or think of a child's fairy story, or of one of the great myths or legends in world literature, which seems in some way to represent your own life. Many psychologists take the view that fairy stories and the great myths and legends contain deep symbolic truths about the human condition, and that it is our conscious or unconscious recognition of these truths that accounts for their perennial popularity.

Don't expect to find a story or a legend that represents your life realistically. Look for symbolic meaning, for a character with whom you feel an affinity, with whom you can identify. It may be Cinderella or King Arthur or

Goldilocks or Orpheus or Isis or Diana, but the important thing is that through your feeling of identification with the character concerned you should feel more able to understand and be in touch with yourself, and to gain strength and insight accordingly.

For those who feel a special affinity with music or with movement, symbolize the way you feel by composing or choosing a piece of music, or by improvising a dance.

It is a sad fact that many of us have become cut off from our own creativity, and thus from a potent source of psychological healing and development. All of us benefit from getting in touch with it.

Jennifer returned again and again to her picture, finding that it revealed more and more about where she was at the time. After a while she identified the smartly dressed woman as the internalized controlling influence of her three older brothers, who always seemed so confident and definite in the way in which they handled their lives. It was the part of her that had been developed by what went on in her life *out there*. The naked woman she saw as the creative side of herself, the *in here* that had never been allowed to reveal itself. Expanding on this interpretation, she then saw the smartly dressed woman as representing her conscious, learnt self, and the naked woman as her unconscious, potential self. Then one day she drew a new picture. This time the smartly dressed woman was looking at the other one with interest, and reaching out a hand towards her.

This new drawing gave Jennifer a sudden insight into her inability to love, and she wrote the following:

Love is creative. Children are conceived through love and should be born into love. Through love, we create a new dimension. The love that we have for each other springs from the same source as the love we have for the world around us, the open sky, the sea on a summer's day, the green grass and cool woods, the soft sound of music, the kiss of the sun, the scent of spring flowers. It stems from the same source that makes men and women want to paint and to write and to bring living shapes into existence from blocks of wood and stone. We share this world with all the forms and colours around us, with everything that moves and lives and breathes. Love stems from the same source as life itself. To love life is to know how to love.

A few days later she added another short paragraph:

I can only love others when I know how to love this creative part of myself, this part of me that loves life. I have to learn how to stretch out a hand to it, like the woman in my picture. I only hope I can do it.

The exercise has helped Jennifer learn a great deal about her current life. By reflecting upon herself, and by using pictures, she has allowed herself to become much more in touch with her own feelings, and to uncover the kind of insights that enabled her to go on from Step 6 to the next steps in her journey.

6

HOW DID YOU GET HERE?

Having answered the question 'Where am I now?' we can now go on to Step 7, 'Find how you got here'. Some psychologists consider this question unimportant. What matters, they argue, is where you are now and where you want to go. But they miss the point that answers to the question 'How did I get here?' are essential for self-understanding. People recognize this for themselves. I have yet to work with anyone tackling psychological problems of the kind discussed in this book who did not have a deep, intuitive awareness of the need to answer 'How did I get here?' if they were ever to know themselves. Nor have I worked with anyone who, once this need was met, did not feel better equipped to make the desired changes in themselves and face the future. Psychologists who ignore this need are a little like the physician who fails to take a case history and to honour the patient's role in his or her own healing.

The importance of answering the question, 'How did I get here?' becomes clearer if we take an analogy from geography. To know that where I am now is Edinburgh as opposed to London or Paris is vital, but I also need to know why I came to Edinburgh rather than London or Paris if I'm going to make the best use of my time here. In the absence of this knowledge, I look around me and see I am in a place called Edinburgh, but my memory for everything that happened up to this moment is unclear. I don't know how I got here and I don't know why I'm here. And if I don't know either of these things, I don't know what is keeping me here should I want to move on, since the things that get us where we are in life are also often the things that hold us captive there.

However, finding out what brought you to where you are now is counterproductive if it leads you simply to blame your present problems upon past history; upon your parents and teachers, for example, and upon the other people who were involved in writing much of the material that went into the early pages of your life script.If you do this you simply write another limiting, over-controlling message in your script that says 'Other people got me into this, it's not up to me to get myself out'. Instead of giving you more power over your life script, this restricts you even further, and may write a further message in the script which says 'I hate the people responsible'. This kind of bitterness not only brings its own kind of suffering, it's also unfair to the people concerned, who, as I mentioned in Chapter 1, may have been victims of their own life scripts – life scripts a lot more difficult, perhaps, than the one they helped write for you.

Bitterness leads us to go on ignoring *in here*. It allocates to the past a control which we should be working at acquiring for ourselves in the present. The result can be feelings of helplessness and despair, and a further loss of autonomy and self-confidence. Quite the opposite of what we want to happen. The purpose of identifying why you are where you are is not to generate bad feelings towards others, but to identify the habits of thinking put there by other people and which have kept you where you are for all too long – so that you can now begin to change.

BRENDA: PERSISTENT SELF-BLAME

Brenda is a good example of the way in which, without a realization of this kind, we can all too easily remain stuck in the programming forced on us by our early script.

When working on Step 6 ('finding out where I am now'), Brenda identified that one of the features of her life is her persistent self-blame. Whenever anything goes wrong with her or with her husband and children she ends up feeling it's her fault, even when it's clear that nothing could be further from the truth. The result is that Brenda spends half her life feeling guilty.

When Brenda examined her relationship with her mother

(pages 89–92) she was surprised at the low rating she gave to it. Up to now she hadn't examined the relationship at all closely, and when asked why, she said this was probably because 'none of us were ever allowed to criticize my mother; she always said we were being disloyal and wicked'. When asked to describe her mother as fully as she could, giving practical examples of her behaviour but without using any value-loaded terms such as 'good' or 'bad', Brenda found herself constantly emphasizing the fact that she had never known her mother admit to being in the wrong. Her mistakes were invariably blamed upon others, even to the point where the whole situation became ludicrous. In Brenda's relationship with her mother, this meant she spent much of her life in the role of culprit and victim, often without any real idea of where she had gone wrong.

Brenda's description of her mother was tape-recorded (a recommended strategy as it helps you go back and reflect upon your material), and played back afterwards. When she heard her own voice detailing the way in which her mother would always shift the blame, Brenda felt a sense of emotional release. For the first time she fully grasped that it was her mother's habit of blaming every mistake on her that was responsible for her own irrational belief that it was always her fault whenever things went wrong. This process of self-blame had started when she was a very small girl, long before she was able to be objective enough to reject her mother's unfair behaviour. And as happens in such cases, this tendency for self-blame had then carried over into other areas of her life. By the time she was older, her script carried the message in bold black ink that whenever anything bad happened, she was the one to blame.

In theory it should have been easy enough for Brenda to work this out for herself years ago. But in reality our early experiences become so built into our identity that we often accept the lessons they teach us without question. It's only when in later life we have the chance properly to distance ourselves, as Brenda did as a result of Step 7, that things become clearer, often to be accompanied by the sense of release experienced by Brenda.

When she talked more about her mother, Brenda admitted that even when things were apparently going well between them she had always felt uneasy when they were together. Now she saw that the reason was because she was always waiting unconsciously for blame of some kind, like bracing herself for a physical blow. By never acknowledging her own mistakes, Brenda's mother had also prevented Brenda from understanding the real relationship between cause and effect, which says 'This went wrong because I forgot to do as I promised', 'That went wrong because you weren't thinking properly', 'This went wrong because he was clumsy', 'That went wrong because she was only thinking of herself', and so on. Right and wrong, blame and responsibility were for Brenda's mother purely emotional matters, unconnected with the facts of the case, and unconnected with proper decisions about who should learn what from a particular mistake, and who should be the one to put it right.

CHRISTINE: RELUCTANCE TO ACKNOWLEDGE MISTAKES

Brenda's mother reminded me very much of Christine, a younger woman with the same reluctance to acknowledge her own mistakes and her own shortcomings. Though in the course of conversation Christine frequently said, 'Of course I know I'm not perfect', she gave very clear indications that in reality she thought she was. She fished for compliments, continually referred to happenings which showed her to good advantage over others, and made it clear that had she wanted to, and had others not denied her her legitimate rights, she would either have married a multimillionaire or become prime minister.

In spite of her conviction that she was one of those upon whom the gods had smiled at birth, Christine suffered from severe bouts of depression, was clearly an under-achiever, and was incapable of keeping friends of either sex for any length of time. Hence her reason for coming to seek help. Not, she made clear, because she needed this help for herself, but because 'I'd like others to understand me better'.

Once Christine's self-investigations began, her progress was rapid, suggesting that part of her had known all along that she was playing to a life script that was more fiction than fact. She identified herself (Step 6, 'where I am now') as a basically insecure person, whose tendency to blame others was really a defence against thinking badly of herself. As part of her life script, she had convinced herself that if she denied responsibility for something, magically it ceased to be her fault. In Step 7 she became aware that the root cause of this conviction was connected with the fact that in the early pages of her script her parents had consistently threatened her with the loss of their love if she was 'naughty'. As a result, she had never been allowed to recognize and accept the fallible side of herself, the side that gets things wrong sometimes, makes a mess of things, behaves badly or irresponsibly or mischievously.

Because she had never been allowed to accept herself unless she was 'perfect', any hint of personal error or inadequacy made her feel vulnerable and insecure. She had defended herself against this by always shifting the blame on to the shoulders of others. Because of their own need to see her as perfect, her parents had been ready to accept this behaviour, no matter how transparent the fantasies it contained. In the end, Christine had found it hard to separate fact from fiction, or to separate what was fair from what was unfair. Distressingly, she was so concerned with her own need for self-defence that this had made her oblivious to the resentment she aroused in other people, in particular in her friends and in family members other than her parents, and oblivious to the fact that this prevented her from building up satisfactory relationships or from making proper use of her real as opposed to her make-believe abilities.

Christine clearly needed to rewrite her life script along more realistic lines. This involved learning a golden rule associated with personal change, namely:

In order to make progress one has first to let go.

Christine had to accept that if she was to change, she had to let go part of the identity her life script had given her. She had to let go the picture of herself as a perfect person, and let go the idea that she could only be loved (and love herself) if she was perfect. She had to let go the old in order to gain the new.

It may sound easy to shed the unwanted parts of your psychological self once you have seen them for what they really are, but this isn't so. The main obstacle is fear. As Christine put it, 'What happens if I lose this "perfect" me? It's who I've been all my life. What can I put in its place? Will there be any of me left?'

Like so many people who start to work on themselves, whether through a therapist or through their own efforts, what Christine wanted deep down was to stay as she was, and yet somehow become miraculously happy – and be *really* successful as opposed simply to fantasizing success. I had to point out to her that that wasn't possible.

The image we used together to overcome this was again the one of travelling. We had established that she was metaphorically in Edinburgh, so that was where the journey had to start. Now we had also established why she was there. She could see that she was carrying a number of enormous bundles marked 'be perfect', and crammed full of useless stuff which made them too bulky to allow her to catch a train or an aeroplane anywhere. Her bundles had kept her rooted to the spot, so to speak. The only solution was to unpack most of them and leave them behind.

Christine found this image helpful. It allowed her to see that the 'perfect' person with whom she had identified was no more her real self than was a suitcase crammed with possessions she no longer needed. She also rather liked the idea of travelling light, and began to realize what an effort it had been for her all her life to convince everyone that nothing was ever her fault and that she was never the one to blame. 'I've been carrying this useless luggage around with me since I was a kid,' she said. 'I can see now how it's got in my way and slowed me down. And I've been so afraid of tripping over it that I've never been able to take risks or go off in a new direction. And because my arms have been full of it I've never been able to get close to anyone else.'

She helped fix this new understanding in her mind by drawing a picture of a woman standing in an airport burdened down with luggage and watching through the window as her flight took off without her. Then she drew a picture of the same woman abandoning her luggage and running easily and lightly towards her departure gate. In the final picture she showed a plane flying above the clouds, and wrote the words 'on my way' underneath it.

EXPLORING YOUR EARLY PAGES

From Chapter 1 onwards you will have started to think about the early pages in your script which were responsible for bringing you to where you are now. Here is an exercise that will help take you further.

▶ Exercise 11: Where your qualities came from

Look again at the six key words you used to describe yourself at the end of Exercise 9 (page 84). Add any other words from Exercise 9 that you wish, and write each word down at the top of a piece of paper.

Now take each word in turn and, whether it suggests a positive or a negative side of you, ask yourself the question 'Where did this quality come from?' Write down on the blank page under the word any answers that come to mind, no matter how bizarre they may seem. You can help yourself by pondering on the following:

* At what age did it first seem to emerge in my life?

* What early examples of my expressing it can I recall?

* Who are the people who most come to mind when I think about it?

* What motives do I have for possessing and using it?

* What incidents in my present-day life prompt me to use it?

If you find it helpful, draw any pictures that come to mind in relation to any of the qualities.

MARTIN, BETTY AND PAUL: THREE DIFFERENT
BACKGROUNDS
For example, when Martin was concentrating on his inability to assert himself, he drew a picture of himself as a young boy lying on the floor and an irate father jumping up and down on him in heavy boots. Betty, concentrating on her violent temper, saw herself as teased and tormented into helpless rage by an older sister and her gang of friends. Paul, concentrating on his dishonesty, drew a picture of himself as a child being hit with a large stick for owning up, and wearing a halo for lying and getting away with it.

None of these three artists had any clear idea of what their pictures were going to represent when they started to draw, and each of them expressed surprise at the results. Martin admitted that he knew his father was a powerful and dominating character, but he hadn't until now realized the extent to which he had felt subdued by him. Betty claimed she had largely 'forgotten' the merciless teasing to which her sister had subjected her over a number of years, while Paul, although he recognized that his clever fibbing had got him out of countless scrapes as a child, confessed he had failed to see that escaping punishment by lying had conditioned him to depend upon dishonesty as a solution to his problems in life. As with most people who work successfully on this exercise, Martin, Betty and Paul found that not only did it bring back long-hidden memories of facts and events, it also prompted them to relive the emotions associated with them. It thus worked at the level of both thoughts and feelings, giving them in consequence particularly sharp insights into the formative influences in their lives.

There is a related exercise that also works at these two levels.

▶ **Exercise 12: Your personal history**

Think carefully about each of the qualities you worked

on in Exercise 11, and ask 'What's the earliest memory I have of this?' Identifying this early memory (or memories) not only helps you understand how the quality became a problem in the first place, but also often unlocks a host of other early feelings and ideas associated with it that have lain concealed for years, and that also help the process of understanding.

You can also use the exercise to get to know more about any side of yourself that you want to understand better. When doing so, people often surprise themselves with the strength with which long-forgotten memories return to them, and with how easy it then becomes to get in touch with the feelings associated with them. When working with 'Being disliked or unpopular' here are some examples of the memories individuals associated with 'My first experience of being rejected':

'Being shut outside the front door by my mother.'

'Walking up and down the hall saying "I don't care" to myself over and over again after I'd been punished.'

'My mother leaving me on my first day at school.'

'Being pulled out to the front of the class by a teacher for something I didn't do.'

'Other children not letting me play with them.'

'Being sent to bed crying in the dark.'

'My mother banging my head against the door knob.'

'Not eating my dinner and having my face pushed in it.'

'Being shaken by my father.'

'Shutting myself in the bathroom and never wanting to come out.'

'Seeing my mother throw on the fire something I'd made for her.'

'Bigger boys hitting me for nothing.'

'Getting work back from a teacher covered in red ink.'

'Having my legs smacked with a stick.'

Memories of the feelings associated with these events included things like 'a red-hot pain in my middle', 'sort of dizzy and choking', 'wanting to curl up and die', 'total annihilation', 'hating everyone', 'as if I couldn't believe it was happening', 'shame and disgrace', 'rage', 'as if I'd lost everything'. Just because we have 'forgotten' events and emotions like this doesn't mean we aren't still carrying them — and their effects — deep down inside us. On remembering and confronting them, some people say the feeling is one of 'exorcism', as if 'something dark and painful and hopeless has been brought into the light and let go'.

LOOKING AT MORE RECENT PAGES

Although events during the early, most formative years of our lives play a big part in getting us to where we are now, they are not the only factors. Although more recent events usually have less of an effect upon the basic way in which we experience the world both *out there* and *in here*, they nevertheless also play an important part in getting us where we are. We may for example have recently chosen an unsatisfactory relationship or an unsuitable job. Or we may have had a recent tragedy in our lives such as a bereavement, or made an error of judgement which has lost us a major opportunity. We may have landed ourselves with too many responsibilities, or responsibilities of the wrong kind. Or we may have failed to satisfy a burning ambition, or have landed ourselves in financial or legal trouble.

There will of course also be many positive things that have happened to us, and many successes and advantages for which we're grateful and which will continue to benefit us in the future. But our main focus is upon the things in our lives with which we're dissatisfied and which we would like to change, the things which have prompted us to experience the psychological difficulties that come between us and the realization of our full potential. Whatever these things are, identifying them in Step 7 allows us to feel lighter and more optimistic about the future. Let's see how one young man got on in Step 7.

RICHARD: A CASE OF STRESS

Richard, a thirty-four-year-old business executive, was suffering badly from the effects of stress. He had had little difficulty in carrying out Step 6. He knew where he was all right, even down to identifying the obsessional symptoms that were creeping into his behaviour, and his irrational, paranoiac fears that everyone was plotting against him both at work and at home ('I frighten myself sometimes with how quickly I get carried away; like some crazy dictator seeing high treason even in his wife and kids'). What he failed to identify was that in his job he had been promoted too far and much too fast. Picked out early as a high-flyer, he had been pushed up the ladder so quickly that before he had time to master one position he found himself several rungs further on.

The result was that Richard felt not only harassed by the pressures of his job but a prey to his own deep insecurity about whether he could really hold it down. His response was to stay later and later at the office, to antagonize his workforce by making impossible demands of them, to take more and more work home in the evenings and at weekends, and to become increasingly estranged from his wife and children.

What had got Richard into this intolerable position was his inability to refuse a promotion before he was ready for it, and his reluctance to protest to his bosses that he needed more support. So much of his self-image was built around (and always had been built around) the idea of being a high-flyer that he couldn't face doing anything that dented it in any way. Fiercely competitive in defence of his high-flyer image, he was quick to be suspicious that others were plotting to take his job if he put so much as a foot wrong, and quick to take his suspicions home with him and project them on to even the innocents in his own family.

Although the things that had brought Richard to where he was were plain for all to see, there was nothing to gain by pointing them out to him directly. People like Richard always learn more quickly when they do things for themselves. Instead, I gave him the next exercise.

▶ **Exercise 13: Identifying negatives and positives**

Select a situation, such as a job or a relationship, which plays an important part in your life today. Write down all the positive things you can think of in connection with it, and all the negative things. Now compare the two lists. What do they tell you?

This is what Richard wrote about his job.

Positive things: status, power, people envy me, importance, get things done, bosses think well of me, achievement, satisfy ambition, workers can't answer back, future prospects.

Negative things: tiring, buck stops here, no time for family, indigestion, incompetent workforce, hostile workforce, need to watch my back, no friends, pulled in all directions.

The nearest he came to admitting what the job was doing to him were in such entries as 'buck stops here' and 'pulled in all directions', but notice that in neither the positive nor the negative entries does he say one word about his feelings. There's no reference to pleasure or to fulfilment, for example. Nor is there anything about stimulus, or challenge. There is no word about value, no word about interest, no word about cooperation. There is nothing about job satisfaction, only about the satisfaction of *ambition*. In short, there is nothing here to suggest that Richard has any liking for his work, or puts anything of his real self into it or gets anything really worthwhile out of it.

On the other hand, there are references to status and power, to what his bosses think of him, and to the way in which he imagines others envy him. This became clear to Richard when he was next asked to underline all words relating first to emotions, then to social factors, then to enjoyment. After puzzling for a moment he admitted he could find none. He was then asked to underline any words that suggested he would be popular with the people who worked under him. Again he could find none. Next I asked him to underline all words that indicated self-centredness, and finally all words that suggested the job was getting on top of him. By the time he had finished these last two tasks there was a line under every word.

The lesson taught by Step 7 was not lost upon Richard and I have more to say about him in Chapter 8.

REPRESSED EMOTIONS AND UNUSED ABILITIES

In Chapter 3 we looked at the part played by your inborn temperament in determining the person you are now. So in answering the question 'How did I get here?' we must take temperamental factors into account. One person is by nature prone to feeling things deeply, another prone to anxiety, another to depression, another to optimism, another to anger, another to humour, another to quick action, another to sociability and so on. There is no simple way to separate out what part of our personality is due to innate temperament and what part is due to life experience, but the former is more implicated in the strength of our emotional responses, and the latter in the kind of things that arouse these responses and in the way we express and use them.

Just because something is in our temperament, it doesn't mean that we actively acknowledge or express it. I stressed in Chapter 3 the importance for our future development of having our emotions accepted by the important people in our lives during our early, most formative years. This need for acceptance continues throughout life since non-acceptance can lead us to repress and ignore an aspect of our temperament that may be very important to our development as a whole human being. (To take extreme examples, imagine how depressing it is to live in an environment where our natural high spirits are constantly condemned as a sign of frivolity and immaturity, or in an environment where our emotional warmth is ridiculed, or where our compassion is dismissed as weakness.)

Answering the question 'How did I get here?' may therefore involve acknowledging aspects of ourselves that so far have not been allowed to emerge. As people put it to me, 'I have this powerful feeling that *something* in me is being wasted', or that 'I have this energy that's never been expressed', or 'I don't feel free inside me'. Like the princess in the fairy tale waiting to be woken with a kiss, there is a strong unsatisfied longing which needs to be recognized and identified.

The same is often true of abilities of one sort or another. We aren't born experts at this or that skill, or this or that art, or this or that science. But we do have differing levels of potential towards them, and if the environment doesn't provide us with the right opportunities, these potentials may lie undeveloped. We may have got where we are now by using our abilities or by failing to use them, and in the event of failing to use them we need to take another look at ourselves and see what is lying fallow.

A two-part exercise that helps us to contact repressed aspects of our temperament and unused aspects of our ability is as follows. Try each part of the exercise at different times. Don't attempt to do them both at one sitting.

▶ **Exercise 14 – part i: Unlocking your temperament**

Temperament. Sit quietly on your own, close your eyes and imagine yourself out in the open, on the seashore or on a mountain or in the countryside, wherever you choose. The sky is blue and clear above you, the air warm, and there is no other person in sight. In your imaginary scene, you can do exactly as you want. You can run, sing, shout, cry, take off your clothes, rage, swim, dance, or just sit and enjoy the peace. What do you choose to do? What are the feelings that prompt you to do it, and how do you feel while you are doing it?

Now you can choose either to bring other people into your picture, or to remain on your own. If you choose other people, who do you choose? What will they be doing? If you choose to remain on your own, how does your solitude feel?

When you have finished this part of the exercise, take a few minutes to ponder what it tells you about yourself. Did you see a familiar side of yourself, or were you surprised by what you decided to do? Did you want to remain on your own, or did you bring in other people? If you did bring them in, who were they? Were they real or imaginary people? There are no right and wrong answers. The point of the exercise is simply to help self-understanding; maybe it didn't throw up any surprises, but maybe it did.

If you had difficulty with the exercise, ask yourself why. Is there something that inhibits you from acting freely, even in the privacy of your own mind? Is it hard to let yourself go? If so, can you discover why? Is there a part of you that is watching another part? If so, what are these different parts? Would it be possible to bring them more closely together?

If during the exercise you brought other people into the picture, why did you choose the individuals concerned? Have they some quality of temperament you would like to have for yourself? Or some quality that you already have and want to express more freely? Do you identify with them in some way? Do they complement something in yourself?

If you chose to remain in solitude, why was this? What is special to you about being alone? Do you often have the chance to enjoy your own company, or are you rarely alone but really would like more time for yourself? If it's the latter, what do you discover about yourself when you're alone that you can't discover when you are with others?

▶ Exercise 14 – part ii: Fulfilled and unfulfilled abilities

Abilities. Again sit quietly on your own, and close your eyes. Take yourself in imagination back to ten years ago (further if you prefer; more recently if your imagination doesn't easily stretch to ten years). Try and recapture how you were at the time. It helps if you can imagine the clothes you might have been wearing, how you would have looked if you had caught sight of yourself in a mirror, how you would have been feeling. When the picture is properly established in your mind, ask yourself where, ten years ago, you hoped or wanted to be today. If you could have seen yourself then as you are now, would you have been satisfied or dissatisfied with yourself, pleased or sorry? If you have missed out on anything you wanted for yourself ten years ago, why is this? What abilities have you been unable to use as you would have wished?

When you have finished this part of the exercise, do as you did with the temperament part, and ponder what it tells you about yourself. Are there abilities in you which have never had a chance to reach their full potential, or abilities which perhaps you have forgotten about altogether over the years? What does thinking about these abilities tell you about the way in which you experience your life now? What lessons does it suggest to you for the future?

At the end of this chapter, we've taken Step 7, which clarifies where you are now, and you're ready to go on to the next stage in the journey, Step 8, 'Find where you want to go'.

PART TWO

BE WHAT YOU WANT

7

WHERE DO YOU
WANT TO GO?

Step 8, 'Find where you want to go', is not as easy as
it sounds. If we have a psychological problem, we like
to imagine simply going to a place where this problem
no longer exists. Of course that isn't possible. Having
psychological problems, or at least meeting the situations
that usually cause problems, is part of being alive. These
situations are not necessarily a bad thing. They provide us
with the challenges and the stimulation that prompt us to
adapt and to grow. We may not enjoy these challenges, but
if we face them in the right way, they provide us with
unique opportunities to learn. And like it or not, life is
one long learning experience, from birth onwards. It is
tempting to think that there is a point at which we will
have 'arrived', a point at which we can 'settle down', and
at which everything else will stay arranged neatly around
us, in much the way that we want it. Such a point doesn't
exist. Life is a constant process of change. The challenge to
us is whether we can learn from the lessons involved in this
change, or whether we allow ourselves to ignore them and
let things run out of control. Life consists of calm periods
and troubled periods, often within the same day or the same
hour, and a life richly lived is a life that can cope with or
accommodate both sets of experiences without undue alarm
or upset.

In Chapter 2 we discussed the fact that the way in which
we experience the world *out there* is very much the result
of the way in which we experience our lives *in here*. The
bottle, you will remember, is either half empty or half full,
depending on how we look at it. In the same way, our
psychological problems are either mountains that loom
intimidatingly over us, or contours that give us a much

better view over the landscape once we get to the top of them.

So the answer to the question 'Where do I want to go?' should not be 'To a place where I'm free of problems', but 'To a place where my problems look different'. If our problems look different, they will seem less like insurmountable obstacles and more like situations with which it is possible to find ways to deal.

JOHN AND MARIA: PROBLEMS BEGIN TO LOOK DIFFERENT

John, a graphic designer who had been working on himself for some months, summed this up when he said, 'I still have my problems, but they don't bother me anywhere near as much now. I suppose you could say it's like having a car that makes strange noises from time to time. You either drive along making yourself neurotic about it, or you accept that a few bumps and rattles are natural in a car that gives you a lot of service. You fix the bumps and rattles that you can, and then accept that as far as the rest are concerned the noise a car makes includes not just the sound of the engine but also the squeaks and grunts of the chassis. That's the natural song of a car. If you don't understand that, you're never going to enjoy driving.'

Maria, attending the same stress management workshop as John, appreciated the car analogy. She said, 'I think of it like driving along and looking at the scenery. I must plan my route as well as I can, and then remember that if I want to get from one place to another it's inevitable that sometimes I'll be looking at the open road and green fields, and other times I'll be looking at traffic and busy streets. But it's all part of the journey. If I'm not prepared for that, I'm being totally unrealistic, and I'll never get anywhere.'

John and Maria have both recognized that in dealing with life we have to realize that it offers both benefits and constraints. There are certain things about it that are as they are and can't be changed by any amount of wishful thinking. (Like the remaining bumps and rattles in John's car or like the traffic and busy streets on Maria's journey. Or like the fact that temperamentally we're never going to be the calm and placid type, or that our abilities are never going to get us the top job, or that we're bound to meet difficulties in any relationship, no matter how good it is.) Life is difficult at times, messy and confusing at times, tiring and frightening at times; but it is also open and joyous at times. In order to love life, we first have to know what it is we are loving, just as in a relationship we first have to know the other person before we can be sure our love is real and not just a passing fancy. To enjoy travelling through your life, you first have to recognize and accept what John calls 'the natural song of the car', and recognize and accept the inevitability of traffic and busy streets as well as the open road and green fields.

In other words, we must change what is going on *in here* if we are to be able to cope with and enjoy and change where necessary what is going on *out there*. So our overall response to the question 'Where do I want to go?' becomes, 'I want to go to a place where *in here* works better for me than it does now, a place where *in here* allows me to accept and tackle realistically what is going on *out there*. A place where *in here* recognizes that I have no magic buttons on my chest just waiting to be pressed by anyone wanting to manipulate my feelings and the way I experience my life.'

This is our overall answer, but we need to add some detail to it. We need to identify the actual things *in here* that have to be changed if we are to reach our destination (or, rather, if we are to make better progress on our journey, for the process of psychological development has no end in our lifetimes). We need to look closely at our life script and see where it has given us the wrong directions for our journey, and where it has loaded us with the excess luggage that Christine saw herself carrying in the last chapter.

▶ Exercise 15: Identifying wrong directions

Read each of the following statements and complete them in your own words.

1. I can only be happy if...
2. I can only be successful if...

 3. Life would be ideal if ....
 4. I feel bad about ....
 5. I wish that ....
 6. I worry most about ....
 7. I'm sorry that I ....
 8. The trouble with other people is ....
 9. It isn't fair on me that ....
10. If I make a mistake it means that ....
11. I'm fearful that ....
12. My opinion of myself depends on ....
13. I can't get over the fact that ....
14. I can't stop thinking about ....
15. What makes me so angry is ....
16. The person who most upsets me is ....
17. I can't feel comfortable unless I ....
18. I just can't handle ....
19. I'm never going to be able to ....
20. There isn't an answer to ....

All the sentences in this exercise have to do with certain
set patterns or habits of thinking which you take from
your life script. They all have to do either with being
manipulated by *out there* ('I can't get over the fact that . . .',
'What makes me so angry is . . .', 'The person who most
upsets me is . . .' and so on), or with wanting to manipulate
it ('I wish that . . .', 'The trouble with other people is . . .',
'I can't feel comfortable unless I . . .' and so on).

When you've completed each of the sentences, what
things do they show you about yourself? How many of these
things about yourself do you want to change? Count them
up and give yourself a total out of 20. Don't automatically
assume that a low total is good and a high total is bad. A
low total may mean simply that you haven't yet accepted
your need to change. A high total may mean that you're
open about yourself or that you recognize there's a lot of
work you want to do. The only purpose of the total is to
help you see things more clearly.

As approaches to life, both vulnerability to being manipulated and our wish to do some manipulating of our own

are unsatisfactory. They suggest the belief that the here and now is never going to be all right until we have got everything arranged just as we think we want it to be. But of course as soon as we get one thing into place, another will slip out of line. It's rather like those little hand-held puzzles with a number of balls which have to be manoeuvred into shallow round holes. You tip the puzzle one way and get some of the balls into place, only to find that when you tip the puzzle the other way to capture the remaining balls, the first ones slip out of position again.

It isn't that we can or should remain immune to what happens *out there*, or that we shouldn't feel the need to change it for the better. But problems arise when what happens *in here* is so over-dependent upon what happens *out there*, that we come to believe our happiness in life depends exclusively upon it. If we're forever in hock to *out there*, we can never be free in our own minds.

WYNN AND MARION: DISCOVERING NEW FREEDOMS
Wynn, a shop manager, put this succinctly when she said, 'I hadn't realized just how much of a prisoner I was inside my own life. I spent so much of my time trying to get everything arranged as I wanted it – first finding someone to marry, then making a home, then trying to have kids, then making a career – that I never had any space to enjoy being alive. I thought happiness depended upon everything else. I didn't realize that the most important thing is an attitude of mind. Get that right, and lots of other things fall into place of their own accord. And even if they don't, you begin to see it isn't necessarily the end of the world. The only person who keeps you prisoner is yourself. You're your own gaoler.'

Wynn found that working on each of the steps we've gone through so far not only led her to a much greater sense of freedom, and of being in control of her own life, but also to a much greater interest in herself as a person. She put it that 'Before I began to think more deeply about myself I hadn't realized how rich and fascinating the human mind is, and what potential there is for self-development. Maybe I should have been a psychologist or a playwright, because the more interesting I find myself, the more interesting I find other people. We're all of us a fascinating study, if we take the time to stop and think about it.'

Wynn's friend Marion, an accountant, noticed the same growing interest in herself as a result of working on the steps covered in this book. 'I've spent years studying and passing exams. I was always good at school, and I got through university with flying colours. The one thing I was never taught to study was myself. I realize now I hardly knew myself, in spite of my university degree and all my certificates and my qualifications. I never realized how fascinating one's own mind actually is.'

Marion, like others who discover this fascination, was quick to point out that it doesn't lead to over-preoccupation with oneself. On the contrary. 'One of the good things about it is that the more you study yourself, the less self-centred you become. I used to be very bound up in myself, without a real clue as to who it was I was bound up in (which is ironic when you come to think about it), but now I'm much more open to others, and more aware and sensitive towards what's happening around me. Being bound up in myself was a sign of insecurity. When you're wrapped up in yourself you worry *about* being worried. You hang on desperately to little bits of yourself in an attempt to hold your life together. You defend yourself like mad, and you don't have much time left over to care about anyone else.'

Wynn agreed. 'In a funny sort of way, I used to think the whole world revolved around me. Now I know it doesn't, and it's such a relief. And, as I said earlier, the more interesting I find myself, the more interesting I find other people. It sounds crazy, but for the first time in my life, I've realized that other people are human beings like me. They all have the same sort of things going on inside their heads, and the same sort of feelings and the same sort of hopes and fears. I can empathize with them much more than I used to, because now I'm getting to know what it's like to be me, I'm getting to know what it must be like to be them.'

IDENTIFYING WHAT NEEDS TO BE CHANGED

Make further progress towards deciding where you want to go by identifying in more detail what you want to change.

▶ **Exercise 16: Things that need changing**

Look back at Exercise 9 in Chapter 5 (page 83). In this exercise you rated yourself on a number of descriptive words, and then wrote a short pen-portrait of yourself based on the most important of them. Which of the characteristics about yourself represented by these descriptive words do you now feel you would like to change? If there is a large number of them – and for many of us there may well be – select the two or three most urgent.

Now ask yourself the following questions about each of them in turn. These questions will help you to discover more about the characteristic concerned, and what has kept it so firmly on the pages of your life script.

1. What particular events typically arouse the characteristic in you?

2. Select a recent example of one such event. What was going through your mind when you responded to it with the characteristic in question?

3. What were the consequences of your response, both in terms of what happened and in terms of how you felt at the time and later?

PATRICIA: WORKING WITH TIMIDITY
Let's look at how Patricia answered each of these questions. Patricia is a sales representative for a large financial planning organization, and finds her job interesting but

stressful. The characteristic she was exploring in herself was 'timidity'.

'I have this picture of myself as a little white mouse, just waiting for other people to pounce on me. I've always had it. It's so well hidden that most people think I'm bursting with confidence. But if they only knew what I go through. I shouldn't really be in a job like mine, where I'm meeting new people and having to convince them to buy financial services from me, but I like the freedom it gives me, and I've always been fascinated by finance. And if I make a success of it, I hope to move into insurance broking where I do less actual selling and more advising.'

In response to question 1, Patricia said: 'Dealing with people who have authority over me. I used to be so terrified of my teachers at school that I'd become tongue-tied if they accused me of anything, and I often ended up getting punished for things that weren't my fault simply because I couldn't speak up for myself. I'm not quite so helpless now on the outside, but on the inside I haven't changed much.'

For question 2, Patricia chose a recent interview with her sales manager, who wanted to talk to her about her disappointing sales record for the previous month. 'I absolutely folded up. There were several good reasons outside my control why I hadn't done well that month, but I couldn't even blurt out one of them. I kept thinking, "He's decided I'm useless. It's all so unfair. He never gives me a chance. He treats me like a child. But I'm not a child. I could do his job much better than he can. I'm much more efficient than he is, and I work a damn sight harder. But no-one takes any notice. I want to just curl up and die."'

Patricia's response to question 3 was, 'He just seemed to treat me with more and more contempt the longer the interview went on. It boosted his ego no end because it cast him in the role of calm efficient boss (which he isn't), and me in the role of dithering idiot – dithering *female* idiot at that. As for me, I couldn't sleep that night, and I worried about it for days afterwards. I kept going over what I *should* have said but didn't. Unless I do some hard thinking about this side of my life, next time he has a go at me I'll probably be even worse.'

In earlier work, Patricia had identified that her timidity was largely learnt in childhood from a mother whom she described as 'frightened of everything that moved'. As a young child, she had been acutely aware of her mother's discomfort in the presence of doctors, teachers, shopkeepers, police officers, traffic wardens, indeed anyone with the remotest pretensions to authority, and equally aware of her mother's horror if her daughter ever tried to stand up to such individuals. 'Mother knew where she and I belonged,' Patricia remarked on one occasion. 'Right at the bottom of the heap.'

As an only-child brought up in a single-parent family, her mother was the only early role-model Patricia had. 'By the time I was old enough to know better, timidity had become so much a part of me that I accepted it without really thinking. I suppose I realized in a sort of way that it was unfair and foolish, but I just lay down underneath it.'

Now let's see what Patricia learnt, in her own words, from her answers to the three questions of a moment ago.

Question 1. 'I think I see the need to re-consider this idea of 'authority'. Up to now I've accepted, more or less without thinking, that 'authority' somehow removes people from the world of mere mortals like me, and turns them into super-beings. I need to recognize that it isn't authority that does this, it's *me*. It's this daft idea I have *about* authority. People with authority are only people, just like the rest of us. I must start seeing them as people, not as powerful ogres. I've been totally unrealistic. And in any case, there are lots of different kinds of authority. I must stop lumping everyone in authority together, and seeing them all as glorified schoolteachers and me as a frightened little schoolgirl.'

Question 2. 'Because of my unrealistic attitude towards authority, I have this irrational belief that my sales manager is a better person than I am, and that my worth as a human being depends upon his thinking well of me. So I would rather be patted on the head by him than make my own assessment of who I am. Whichever way you look at it, that's just plain stupid.'

Question 3. 'It's stupider still that through being so dependent upon what he thinks about me, I let myself sink even lower in his estimation. And by boosting his ego, I'm making him even more insufferable in the future. The sort of feelings I had when he was talking to me were exactly the same as the ones I used to have when someone told me off at school. Feeling that way is just a habit. And each time I indulge in it, I just feed it and make it stronger next time.'

Patricia thus identified a number of things that needed to be changed in her present behaviour.

1. She realized that she was not looking realistically at the real meaning of 'authority'. Her life script had left her with the message that she had to go in fear and trembling of anyone with the slightest claim to this 'authority'. The script had thus prevented her from being objective in her attitude towards the people concerned.

Patricia's situation is a very common one. We all need from time to time to re-examine the important concepts we hold in our lives. These concepts might be 'authority' as in Patricia's case, or things like 'duty', 'conscience', 'guilt', 'belief', 'religion', 'power', 'status', 'pride', 'obey' – even 'love' – to name but a few. We often carry such concepts in our minds in almost exactly the form they were when given to us by others. They profoundly affect the way in which we approach and experience our lives, as Patricia discovered. Yet it is only when we begin to think about the meaning they have for us *personally* that we can come properly to own them for ourselves. Often we make the discovery that this personal meaning is very different from the meaning given to us by others, and this discovery can radically alter the way in which we think about existence and our own place within it. It can help us throw away much useless baggage.

2. Patricia learnt that she was more dependent upon the approval of others than upon her own realistic

assessment of her worth. Even when the person offering the approval was someone – like her sales manager – for whom she had little real respect.

Patricia therefore was acknowledging that, again like so many of us, she was in no real sense her own person. How could she be, when her opinion of herself was under the control even of people she knew to be less efficient than herself? Her self-esteem went up and down in direct response to the way others treated her, instead of in response to her estimation of her own worth. Instead of teaching her how to be *self-rewarded*, her life-script had taught her only to be *other-rewarded*. Recognizing the extent to which our life script can place us in hock to other people is a vital step in identifying what changes we should make in our lives so as to establish a more equal balance between rewards generated *in here* and rewards generated *out there*.

3. **Patricia recognized that her behaviour was self-defeating. By being overawed when in the presence of 'authority' she was in fact producing the very impression that she wanted to avoid, namely that she was a 'dithering female idiot'. The more subservient and tongue-tied she became, the more superior and contemptuous became her boss.**

It's a fact of life that some people become increasingly overbearing if others cave in to them. Patricia's boss is clearly one of these people. Patricia had a perfectly reasonable explanation for her below-average sales performance of the previous month, and she had a perfect right to let her boss know about it. By not doing so she simply strengthened him in his wrong impression of her, an impression which implied, incidentally, a strong hint of sexism in addition to some pretty poor professional judgement, and which showed the extent to which, like many similar people, he was playing out his immaturity, ego problems, and professional inadequacies on others. In other words, he was making others a victim of his own problems, and Patricia was unwittingly offering herself as a very real victim indeed. By boosting his very immature ego, she was feeding his problems and making life more difficult for herself in the future.

SELF-ESTEEM AND SUCCESS OR FAILURE

Patricia provides us with an example of the vital point that when identifying the ways in which they want to change, most people recognize as an important underlying issue the *wish to think well of themselves*. Provided we think well of ourselves, we are able to cope with the great majority of the psychological problems that life puts in our path.

When I referred earlier to thinking well of oneself – self-esteem – I stressed that this has nothing to do with conceit (page 48). Conceit – irrespective of whether or not there is anything to be conceited about – is more often than not a sign of deep insecurity. Typically, conceited people can only think well of themselves if others share their own high opinion of their worth. Whenever we meet with someone who has to keep telling the world how marvellous they are, we can suspect a deep inner problem, a problem which becomes only too evident when the person concerned, for whatever reason, loses his or her status. The result of this loss is deflation, diminution of identity, and sometimes even complete personal collapse.

In contrast to conceit, self-esteem has to do with the recognition that everybody, oneself included, is worthy of respect simply by virtue of their humanity. It leads to (and can be recognized by) a feeling of *befriending*. We become friends with ourselves. That doesn't mean we can't be self-critical or see the need to change certain aspects of ourselves. It doesn't mean we become complacent and self-indulgent. It means that we give ourselves the support and the understanding that we extend to our best friends, and also that we show the openness and honesty towards ourselves that we show towards them. It means that, unlike

Patricia, we are *self-rewarded* as well as *other-rewarded*, in other words, that we value ourselves enough to value our own opinions about ourselves and our lives. It means that we extend compassion and consideration towards ourselves in the same way that we extend them towards others, and that we encourage ourselves and believe in ourselves in the same way we can encourage and believe in others.

It was a very wise psychologist who told us to love our neighbours as ourselves. Not more than ourselves, not less than ourselves, but *as* ourselves. One of the profound implications behind this teaching – an implication all too often ignored by those who go in for much self-guilt and self-abasement – is that our love for ourselves is a yardstick for our love for others. Unless we can love ourselves, it is doubtful whether we can truly love anyone else.

Present day psychology bears out this teaching. The evidence suggests strongly that unless we learn the value and the meaning of love *in here*, it is very difficult to extend it properly *out there*. Our love for others, if we are at odds with ourself, is all too often characterized by possessiveness, by insecurity, and by a desperate personal need for what one gets *from* the love rather than for what one puts into it. Love of this kind has an immaturity about it, a self-centredness, and very often a fantasy element which decrees the other person cannot be loved for who they are but only for who we would have them be.

Self-esteem – the ability to extend this love to ourselves – depends importantly upon experiencing our lives through success rather than through failure, and we will return to this issue in the next chapter. For the moment, though, if you cast your mind back to one of the most formative influences in your life, your schooling – you will recognize that much of it was judged by failure rather than success. It is a sad fact that the education system emphasizes what we can't do rather than what we can, our mistakes rather than our achievements, what we get wrong rather than what we get right, and, moreover, emphasizes these things in a negative and unhelpful way. Instead of teaching us that the things we can't do help us recognize where we need to go next, that making mistakes is a natural and often essential part of the learning process, and that getting things wrong is not a reason for punishment but for recognizing where we require guidance and help, it is implied that they add up to a picture of personal incompetence which renders us very inadequate members of the human race.

Even the people who experience more success than failure may be adversely affected, if success at school demands a continuous diet of good results in order to continue to be regarded as success. If you have been taught that self-worth is geared to externally imposed assessments, to good marks and good grades and to the prizes that go with them, the constant need to 'prove' yourself can remain throughout life.

MORE ABOUT SUCCESS AND FAILURE

When people who claim they see themselves as 'failures' in life are asked to explain what they mean, they come up with statements like 'I set myself goals and I never reached them', 'Other people expected so much of me, and I've let them down', 'I'm just so disappointed with myself all the time', 'I've wasted my life', 'Other people think I'm useless', 'I just can't cope with life', 'I'm no good at *anything*'. The most helpful response to these statements of defeat is to ask the individual concerned questions designed to help him or her look more closely at what they have just said. Questions such as:

'Were the goals you set yourself realistic?'

'Were they really your goals, or did you take them over from other people?'

'Why do you suppose other people's expectations of you were the right ones?'

'What realistically would you need to be able to achieve in order to stop being disappointed with yourself/to stop feeling you've wasted your life/to feel you can cope with life?'

'Why are other people's judgements of you more important than your own?'

'What standards would you need to reach in order to feel you *are* good at something?'

Questions of this kind don't produce magic answers, but they do help the individual to start examining some of his or her assumptions. It's sometimes all too easy to become trapped into the idea of 'failure', taken over from the judgements of others or from an unrealistic assessment of what is possible and of what one can realistically expect of oneself.

Failure for the most part breeds failure, just as success for the most part breeds success. There is a very simple but vital rule for anyone falling behind in the tasks they or others set for themselves. It is that they need to experience success *at no matter how basic a level*. If they can set themselves or be set challenges which they can realistically meet, their self-belief will increase and the level of difficulty facing them can then be progressively increased. When this rule is observed for example with children, the results are always good, and often outstanding. The children concerned have been failing largely because they have been taught to see themselves as failures. Once they are allowed to experience success, and thus to see themselves as successes, they start to succeed.

By identifying what one realistically means by success, and what tasks one needs to undertake in order to achieve it, and by tackling these tasks in small steps and noting each success instead of dwelling on each failure, one progressively improves not only one's skills but crucially one's belief in one's own ability.

The next exercise will help you recognize how your concept of success and failure, as written into your life script by your early experiences, is influencing your attitude to your life and your life experiences today.

▶ **Exercise 17: Success and failure**

Think carefully about each of the following questions. Try to base your answers to them upon specific examples of your own behaviour.

1. *Do you judge your abilities on short-term or long-term evidence?* For example, does one 'bad' performance at something make you feel inadequate, or can you take it in your stride if you've been successful at other times?

2. *Do you tend to prejudge your performance at something new even when you've no evidence on which to go, or do you wait and see how you get on before coming to any conclusions?*

3. *Do you hold generalized views of your abilities* (for example, 'I'm no good at anything to do with numbers', 'I'm hopeless at making friends', 'I've got an appalling memory') *or do you think of them in more specific terms?* ('I can handle simple arithmetic but I'm lost if it gets too complex', 'I've made some close friends in my life but I don't always find friendship easy', 'I've a good memory for anything unusual but I'm less good when it comes to routine matters'.)

4. *Do you tend to make statements in terms of your shortcomings, or in terms of what you should do to overcome them?* For example, 'I'm no good at handling people' rather than 'I need more practice at handling people'; 'I don't always find friendship easy' rather than 'If I could be a better listener I'd find friendship much easier'; 'I just can't seem to remember facts and figures' rather than 'I should concentrate more if I want to be better at remembering facts and figures'?

5. *Do you tend to personalize mishaps, and frequently end up blaming yourself for things outside your*

control, or can you be more objective? For example, you arrange a dinner party and a sudden power cut ruins the preparation of the main course; do you blame yourself for having been 'silly enough to plan such an elaborate meal', or blame yourself by ascribing it to 'just my luck'? Or do you accept that since power cuts happen so seldom you were perfectly justified in assuming there wouldn't be one that evening?

6. *Do you tend to think in terms of extremes (things are either right or wrong, good or bad, black or white) or are you able to recognize the middle ground?* (There are two sides to most questions, all factors should be taken into account, balance is necessary.)

7. *Do you exaggerate the importance of minor mishaps, or do you keep a sense of proportion?* For example, do you think people will think badly of you for a small social gaffe, or worry that a friend will hold it against you for having your say, or for being five minutes late, or for forgetting a birthday?

8. *Do you find yourself apologizing for the least little thing* (an accidental brush of shoulders with a colleague in a busy corridor, using the phone or a photocopier when another person arrives wanting to use it, making an unavoidable error) *or do you recognize that apologies aren't called for at such times?*

9. *On the other hand, do you find it difficult to apologize even when you are in the wrong, afraid that admitting errors diminishes you in your own eyes and other people's? Or do you recognize that no-one is infallible, and that accepting our mistakes is a sign of strength.*

If you've answered 'yes' to the first part of any of these

nine questions, you've identified areas where you tend to think of yourself in terms of failure rather than in terms of success. You should now be able to see where you need to change if you are to raise your self-esteem to where it belongs.

Having worked through Step 8, 'Where do I want to go?', we are now ready to move to Step 9, 'How to get there?', that is, how to make the changes you've identified as important to you.

8

HOW TO GET THERE

Let's recap briefly on the eight steps you have taken so far.

Step 1 helped you see the lack of real control most of us have over our thoughts and our emotions. Our heads and our hearts seem to have a will of their own, and to push thoughts and feelings into our consciousness much as they please.

Step 2 involved the recognition that once we acknowledge this lack of control, we need to ask what in our life experience has prompted us to have the kind of thoughts and feelings we do, so that we can then start to change them in ways that will help us live more fulfilled and contented lives.

Steps 3 and 4 enabled us to recognize firstly that, given the scant help most of us received on how to be in charge of our inner lives, there's no point blaming ourselves if we're not very good at it; and secondly that the possession of psychological problems isn't a sign of weakness. Steps 3 and 4 helped you see your life in terms of a *life script*, many of the chapters of which were largely written for you by others before you knew enough to be able to write them for yourself, and which lays down the way in which you experience your own being.

Step 5 brought you to the realization that in spite of the lack of help we've received in taking charge of our inner lives, we do have the power to change them for ourselves. No-*one* and no *thing* in the world *out there* can directly affect our psychological life *in here*. There are no magic buttons on our chests for the people and events in the outside world to press in order to make us think or feel as we do. In the final analysis, it is we who do things to ourselves. We each of us interpret the world and our own experiences of it in our own subjective way. No matter how strong the teaching of our life script, once we recognize this and are helped to understand ourselves better and use ourselves in a psychologically more effective manner, we can start reshaping our lives more as we want them to be.

Step 6 involved looking closely at where you are now. Only by looking at the way in which we see ourselves and the way in which others see us, and by examining our relationships with parents, partners and the other significant people in our lives, can we get an accurate idea of what is happening to us. We may know well enough whether we are happy or not, but most of us never stop to take a hard look at the various details in our lives that have a bearing upon this happiness or the lack of it.

Step 7 involved looking equally closely at how you got here. The point was stressed that a knowledge of the influences that have made us what we are is vital for self-understanding. Failure to gain this knowledge is like opening an unfamiliar book in the middle pages and being told to write the next chapter. There is a very old Celtic saying that 'people have to know where they are coming from if they are to know where they are going'. And although there is no need to know our personal psychological history in great detail, we need a general picture of its influence upon us if we are to understand and take some control of the life script it has written for us.

Step 8 brought us to an identification of the kind of changes we want to make in our lives. We cannot escape to a place where there are no psychological problems, since to be alive is to face problems. But we can find our way to a place where we see these problems in a different light, a place where we know how to handle them and where they trouble us less. A place in fact where we can reinterpret the way in which we see, relate to, and cope with the world.

SOME PREPARATIONS

Each of these first eight steps contains an element of Step 9, 'Make the changes you want'. By recognizing and understanding the ideas and the techniques and the practices associated with Steps 1-8, we have already started to make these changes, to embark on the journey to where we want to be. The first eight steps are highly active and productive ones (hence the term 'steps'), and taking each of them changes our lives in fundamental and long-term ways. But Step 9, the one we are going to take in this and the next chapter, is the most active and productive of all.

It also involves the highest level of commitment. As the changes in yourself go deeper and deeper, they will become more noticeable to others, and you may meet resistance from them. This is because change is sometimes uncomfortable. It is human nature to become accustomed to the status quo, since it provides a certain sense of security, and allows people to feel they can predict and understand the things that happen. Change unsettles the picture, and can therefore make them feel less sure of themselves, more vulnerable. When we change, we can also affect other people more directly, in that our previous behaviour may have been very convenient for them, whereas our new-found independence, or self-assurance, or change of career, or change of direction may fit less well with their plans or their way of life. Changes in us may also prompt them to look more closely at their own lives, and see perhaps that there are changes which they in turn should make, but the need for which they have long ignored or resisted.

Within close relationships, change may mean that people have to get to know new aspects of each other and adjust to new qualities. The result may be a certain coolness in these relationships, until a new understanding brings with it a new warmth or a new honesty. And change can also be challenging for us ourselves, in that we also will have become accustomed to things as they were, no matter how unsatisfactory, and in that we also may feel a little insecure about the new directions our lives are taking.

It is, however, important not to feel intimidated. Life changes anyway, all the time. You are not inventing the idea of change, simply taking more control over the form change is going to take. Naturally and rightly, you will want to study the needs of others in your life and avoid changes that will bring unnecessary disruption or distress. But it is equally important not to be too easily daunted by obstacles that from time to time will inevitably appear in your path. Each obstacle is a new teacher, and as you learn from it you gain new wisdom and strength to continue.

In addition, be prepared for some ups and downs. It's natural to suppose that psychology is rather like medicine: you have something wrong, you take the necessary remedy, and that's the end of the matter. But it doesn't work that way. The human mind and emotions are complex things. Once you start the process of change and meet with results, you may conclude that everything is now going to be fine, and that you're never going to feel like your old troubled self again. Then one morning you wake up feeling – perhaps for no apparent reason – as bad as you used to. Or some unexpected difficulty occurs, and you find all the old anxieties resurfacing. As a result you feel acute disappointment, and conclude that the good feelings you were experiencing were just an illusion.

This is a danger period. It's easy to lose heart at this point, but this is the one thing you must never do. The good feelings weren't an illusion. To assume that they were, and that the bad old times are back to stay, is an example of what psychologists call a *maladaptive* thought. It misreads the present situation, interpreting it in terms of the old life script instead of in terms of current reality. The good feelings indicated to you, clearly and unequivocally, that you have the capacity within yourself to feel confident and at ease; if you continue with your work on yourself, they will return as surely as they arose in the first place. It's a question of having the patience and the motivation to keep going forward, instead of allowing yourself to slip back into a way of life dictated for you by a life script which has now become old and obsolete.

Dealing with the Downs

One way to keep going when you meet a bad period is to refuse to identify with the negative bad feelings that resurface. Usually what happens when we feel bad is that in a significant sense we *become* our bad feelings. They dominate us because we've never been taught – or we've forgotten – that there are other kinds of feelings apart from the ones we've got at the moment. We wake in the morning with a heavy feeling in the stomach, or we're filled with a hot twist of panic when something threatens us either from *in here* or *out there*, and we feel helpless in the face of it, as if it is going to dominate our whole life. But keep these feelings in perspective by just observing and noting them, in the way that, for example, you observe and note that it's raining outside, and then turn your attention to more important matters and get on with your life.

Help yourself through a bad patch as well by returning to a modified form of Exercise 1.

▶ **Exercise 18: You are not your thoughts or emotions**

Sit comfortably and close your eyes. Relax any tension you feel in any part of your body, and let your breathing come from as deep in the abdomen as possible. Let your mind stay empty, but keep alert. Don't doze or drift into sleep. When a thought or an emotion arises, just observe it, and observe any other thoughts or emotions set off by it. Notice that you don't have to become part of it. Let it pass in and out of your awareness like a cloud crossing the face of the sky. Notice that you are *not* your thoughts and you are *not* your emotions. These are simply things that happen, temporary things that only have the meaning you choose to give them. Don't make an effort to ignore them, to push them away, or to prevent them from arising. This only increases their hold over you. Just observe them in a detached way, and let them go.

Continue this exercise for a few minutes, then gently open your eyes. Retain the realization that you are your own person, that you don't have to be dictated to and manipulated by passing thoughts and emotions *in here*, any more than you have to be dictated to and manipulated by events in the world *out there*.

Try to practise this exercise regularly. Set aside a few minutes each day for it, preferably at the same time and in the same place. Choose a time and place when you are unlikely to be interrupted. You can carry out the exercise at other times too, particularly at moments when you feel tense or in low spirits. Practised over a period, it will deepen your conviction that you are not at the mercy of your chatterbox of a mind or of the changing panorama of your emotions.

Practise the exercise in conjunction with the relaxation exercise given on page 217, which will further help you with the technique of observing the distance that exists between who *you* are and the temporary thoughts and feelings that arise in the mind and the body.

Recording Your Progress

Now we need to return to another of the earlier exercises, Exercise 7 in Chapter 2 (see page 34), where you kept a record of your state of mind over a period of time. Keeping a record in this way is one of the best methods not only for getting more in touch with your feelings (in other words recognizing and accepting them) but also for observing the fact that these feelings are not *you* but *things that happen to you*. How could they be you, when they come and go while *you* are there all the time?

Notice from your record how your moods rise and fall, how your state of mind changes from hour to hour and from day to day. Note also what things *out there* prompt this rise and fall and this change from hour to hour. Since there are no magic buttons for these things to press, note what it is in you that makes you respond in the way you do. What aspect of yourself is put under threat by the things concerned? By the end of Chapter 7 you will already have identified those of your attributes that you want to change; now start watching for the occurrence of these attributes. They are nothing to be ashamed of. It is vital that we get to know more about them. No good will come of trying to turn our back upon them.

Step 9 consists of four separate tasks, and we shall meet them one by one as we go through the chapter. But the first of them is in fact the one I have just been describing. We can state it like this:

* recognize and be more in touch with your feelings and your states of mind.

* accept that although they happen to you, these feelings and states of mind are temporary and are not who you really are.

* accept that as negative feelings and negative states of mind arise largely in response to a life script heavily influenced by others, you must take over the writing of the life script so that these negative feelings and states of mind trouble you less, and arise less and less often.

The second task in Step 9 follows on from Task 1, and involves noting what things *in here* prompt the rise and fall of your moods and states of mind. The life script has programmed you to react to events *out there* by thinking about them in a certain way. The thought or thoughts concerned then prompt your emotional response or your mood or your subsequent state of mind. The nature of your initial thought or thoughts must therefore be identified if you want to influence the way in which you are reacting. So the second task is as follows.

* recognize the negative thought or thoughts, put there by your life script, that arises in response to external events.

* accept that this thought (or thoughts) is the product of an outdated life script and is a maladaptive way of responding to present reality.

PHILIP

Philip, whom we met in Chapter 2, is a good example of how this works in practice. Philip described himself as 'a very anxious sort of person – in a perpetual state of near bloody panic', yet when he was asked to keep a written record of his state of mind every hour on the hour for an average week, he found that the non-anxious times clearly outnumbered the anxious ones. On the strength of this he was forced to conclude that it was more accurate to describe himself as 'a very anxious sort of person *some* of the time'. Or, to put it more positively, as 'an unanxious person *most* of the time'.

Keeping a written record of his state of mind enabled Philip to recognize that *because* he had grown to think of himself as a very anxious person, he had got into the habit of becoming acutely self-aware during his anxious moments, and letting the much more numerous non-anxious moments pass virtually unnoticed. As I said in Chapter 2, this is a classic case of selective attention. Part of Philip's solution was to become more self-aware during the good times, and thus to put the anxious moments into proper perspective. But in accordance with Task 2 in Step 9 he also started work on recognizing the unspoken thought or train of thought that sparked off his anxiety, and thus was able to tackle his anxiety states more directly.

At first, Philip denied there *were* such unspoken thoughts. As he put it, 'Something happens, like getting called in unexpectedly to see my boss at work, and I feel a bloody great wave of anxiety before I've had time even to take a breath, let alone start thinking.' But once Philip's attention was drawn to the need to observe himself more closely at the moment his wave of anxiety surged through him, he found to his surprise there *were* unspoken thoughts there, and clear ones at that. In his own words, 'The thoughts are always along the lines of "Something awful is going to happen". Once I started to watch out for them, I was amazed I hadn't seen them properly before. I suppose I'd just got so used to them.'

TRIGGER THOUGHTS

Philip's case is typical. Once we look closely at ourselves at the moment when an unwanted emotion surfaces – whether it be fear or anger or anxiety or sadness or obsessional feelings or whatever – we see that most of the time a thought exists (or existed in the past when that particular emotion first became a problem, and can be retrieved from the memory) between the outside event and the emotion. It is a thought (or thoughts) put there by our life script, and which over the years has become virtually automatic. Such thoughts are sometimes called 'precipitating thoughts' by psychologists, but I prefer the term 'trigger thoughts', since it is these thoughts that usually trigger off the feelings or the states of mind which form our problem. *These thoughts are the nearest things to magic buttons*, and it is aspects of these thoughts that you must change as you learn to take over the writing of your life script for yourself. (I have more to say about the nature of these thoughts in Exercise 19 later on.)

Of course, not all trigger thoughts are bad. Much of our desirable behaviour is sparked off by them as well. Although unrecognized trigger thoughts lie behind our words when we say such things as 'On impulse, I just went and helped', or 'Without thinking I spoke up for myself', or 'I just had to do something for him/her', or 'I saw the bus and I ran for it', or 'The moment the bell went I was out of the door'. In all such cases, our motivation to action indeed depends upon these thoughts.

In Philip's case, the trigger thought each time his boss summoned him was that something unpleasant lay in store, and his anxiety was immediately aroused. In the case of someone whose problem is anger, the trigger thought might be 'I must hit back', or 'I must make you do as I say', or 'She's getting the credit that belongs to me', or 'He's flirting with my wife'. In the case of sadness there's often a trigger thought to do with loss: 'Those good times are gone', 'She doesn't love me any more', 'I've lost my chance', 'I'm growing old', 'My life is so lonely now the children are grown up'.

In spite of the fact that many of us would say, like Philip, that the wave of emotion comes over us before we have time to think about anything, we will nevertheless find – again like Philip – that on the great majority of occasions there is indeed a trigger thought associated in some way with it, and that it usually doesn't take much special attention to spot it. When we've spotted it once or twice, it becomes increasingly easy to do so on subsequent occasions. Many people attest to a feeling of relief once they're able to identify their trigger thoughts in this way. It makes it much easier for them to recognize that what's happening when the unwanted emotion arises is that they're playing out the routine of their outdated life script. In other words, they find it easier to recognize that because in the past particular experiences led to emotionally unpleasant outcomes, their life script has given them patterns of thought that suggest to them that similar outcomes will continue to happen, no matter how different the circumstances under which they live their lives.

This brings us to the third task in Step 9.

* **Having identified the trigger thought(s), deal with it, and rob it of its power.**

How do you do this? Simply identifying it helps. Philip said, 'I used to feel as if my anxious moods were caused by other people or events, or just came out of the blue, and that they were completely outside my control. Recognizing there were no magic buttons on my chest put other people and events into perspective, and so took me half way towards seeing how mistaken this was. Identifying my trigger thoughts took me the rest of the way by dismissing the notion of 'out of the blue'. What seemed incomprehensible became clear and very simple.'

But we can go further than this. Let's stay a little longer with the example of Philip. When working on Step 7, 'How Did I Get Here?', Philip identified that his tendency to anxiety was linked to the fact that when he was five years old he had lost his much-loved father in a road accident. Soon afterwards, his mother had fallen seriously ill, and remained a semi-invalid throughout the rest of his childhood, with recurring crises which entailed her being rushed off to hospital at a moment's notice, often in the middle of the night.

An only-child, his mother's precarious hold on life had represented Philip's sole security, and not surprisingly his existence in consequence had seemed poised always on the brink of tragedy, programming him to expect the worst. Thus even when he reached adulthood, any non-routine event, such as being summoned to a meeting with his boss, produced the trigger thought 'Something is wrong; something bad is going to happen'.

HOW TRIGGER THOUGHTS COME ABOUT

It's useful to give another extended example of how trigger thoughts arise in the first place. Although initially based upon actual events, notice how such thoughts take on a conditioned, mechanical quality, particularly if the emotion connected with them is a very strong one.

If your problem is a fear of speaking in public, for instance, you may as a child or as an adolescent have been ridiculed by a teacher or by other children on being asked to stand up and say something in front of the rest of the class. After several incidents of this kind (or a single and very traumatic one) the trigger thought 'I shall be laughed at/punished/make a mess of it' arises each time the thought of public speaking crosses your mind or you are actually called upon to speak in front of others, and triggers off your fear. The presence of this fear makes you even more likely to fail, and the trigger thoughts and consequent emotion become ever more deeply ingrained.

Another possibility is that before public occasions you had it impressed on you that parents or teachers expected much, and that bad behaviour or a bad performance would shame and disappoint everyone. The result was that you became so nervous that failure, and consequent recriminations, became inevitable.

A fear of speaking in public can of course arise for the first time in adult life, though this is less usual. Here again, the causes are similar. You have one or two traumatic experiences of apparent failure, or feel you have let others down, or receive hypercritical comments, and the trigger thoughts 'I can't do this', 'I shall fail again' resurface each time public speaking is required in the future.

As in most areas of human behaviour, temperament also plays a part, of course. Some individuals, more sensitive by nature than others, are more likely to be wounded by humiliating experiences and therefore more likely to develop consequent trigger thoughts. We can see this equally clearly if we look at the example of anger. Some people have temperaments which are more quickly aroused than others, which makes them in turn more likely to react to threats to themselves or their possessions or status.

But an easily aroused temperament doesn't necessarily make one an irritable, irascible person. It is environment that ensures it develops in that direction, for example an environment where you are constantly called upon to defend your status or your self-esteem, or where other people delight in teasing and baiting you, or where frustrations abound, or where your upbringing teaches you that you must always 'get even' with others. The trigger thoughts 'I *won't* let them take this from me', 'How *dare* they put me down', 'I *must* get my own back' and so on quickly become established.

Once such trigger thoughts are recognized, we can start to work on them. Unrecognized, they can all too easily dominate our lives for us.

Re-evaluating Your Trigger Thoughts

The lessons learnt in Step 7 can now be used to help us *re-evaluate* our trigger thoughts. Our life script has taught us at an impressionable point in our lives that these thoughts are valid, and consequently we have gone on thinking them over the years in spite of subsequent evidence that often they are not valid at all. Once we realize that they are there, not because they represent an accurate appraisal of reality, but because they are part of our outdated script, we can begin this process of *re-evaluation*.

Re-evaluation is made easier as a result of practising Exercise 18 above. Exercise 18 was intended to help you observe the distance that exists between who you are and the temporary thoughts and feelings that arise in your mind and body. It helped you see that you don't have to identify with these thoughts or feelings, since their temporary nature indicates they are not who you really are. Once you cease to identify so wholeheartedly with your thoughts – and in particular with your trigger thoughts – you can also begin to examine them more objectively, and assess whether they contain truths relevant to your life as you live it now.

Going back once more to Philip, and taking as our example his surge of anxiety each time his boss asked unexpectedly to see him, we can appreciate how this re-evaluation works. Philip's trigger thought on being summoned into the presence of his boss was 'Something is wrong; something bad is going to happen'. But when he began to look at this thought objectively, he saw that it bore little relation to the real facts of the matter. His boss was usually a reasonable man, and when he asked to see Philip unexpectedly it was generally for nothing more threatening than to ask for information or advice which Philip was more than able to give. Philip was good at his job, and there were several signs that his boss was aware of this and esteemed Philip accordingly.

Working this out for himself, Philip saw that his trigger thought, 'Something is wrong; something bad is going to happen', was related to events back in the past when his mother had called him in the night to say she was ill again, or when a teacher or someone else in authority had summoned him to give him the news that she had been taken abruptly into hospital. These past events had nothing to do with the present, or with the situation that existed between Philip and his boss. Recognizing this didn't put an immediate end to Philip's anxious trigger thoughts. They were too habitual for that. But it allowed him to see them for what they were, and thus to relax more when they arose, and begin to rob them of their power.

It isn't usually necessary to identify *specific* events in the past, as in Philip's case. It is often quite enough to identify the trigger thought as related in a general way to one's past life experience (for example that pessimistic trigger thoughts are related to the pessimistic view of life taken by one's parents, or that trigger thoughts to the effect that 'I must always take charge' are related to the responsibilities one was forced to assume as the oldest child in the family). The important thing is to perceive the distance between this past experience and what is happening *now*. The trigger thought is more often than not no longer appropriate. Whatever usefulness it may have had is probably long since over. It is time to take more control *in here*, and, by refusing to identify habitually with the trigger thought, to divest it of its power over your emotional life.

Philip's feeling of anxiety at being called in to see his boss was essentially a private thing. It was an issue between him and himself, rather than between him and another person. But inappropriate trigger thoughts can equally well be set off in social situations where we misread the motives or intentions of others by responding to them in terms of an outdated life script instead of in terms of current realities.

RICHARD

Exercises 2, 3 and 4 in Chapter 2 (pages 22-4) helped us see how subjective we are in the way in which we experience and interpret the world. We each of us build up this personal way of experiencing and interpreting as a result of our life script. Where our life script is faulty, then all too often so is our experiencing and interpreting. In the case of Richard in Chapter 6 we saw a man who had come to believe he was only acceptable to others if he could hang on to his 'high-flyer' image. He thus couldn't face doing anything that dented this image in any way. Fiercely competitive in defence of it, he was quick to be suspicious that others were plotting to take his job if he put so much as a foot wrong. And quick to carry his suspicions home with him, and imagine that his family were plotting against him as well.

Working subsequently on Step 9, Richard identified that when dealing with his colleagues the trigger thoughts 'This person is threatening my status', or 'They're all just waiting to stab me in the back', or 'This person is after my job' frequently caused him to put pressure on himself and to react with anger to others. Once he started to analyse these thoughts, Richard recognized that they had much more to do with demands put upon him during his boyhood by parents and teachers that he keep proving himself when a boy than with his present situation in life. He was interpreting the intentions of his present colleagues and superiors in terms of motives held towards him in quite different circumstances by quite different people at a quite different stage of his life.

Understanding this, Richard found the old trigger thoughts beginning to lose their power. Able now to be more objective, he found that, despite the small jealousies that occur whenever people work together, the overriding concern of his colleagues and superiors was in fact with the success of the organization, since all their livelihoods depended upon it. Supporting Richard was far more important to them than seeing him fail. Once he fully understood this, the result was that Richard found much of the pressure lifted from his shoulders. It was pressure put there not by others but by himself.

TANIA AND MICHAEL

If we look again at the case of Tania and Michael in Chapter 5, we can see how inappropriate trigger thoughts can work to damage relationships. Tania's problem was that Michael left everything to do with their two young children to her, with the result that she felt exploited and increasingly disenchanted with him. Tania and Michael subsequently agreed to work on this problem together, and when discussing Step 7, 'How Did I Get Here?', Michael confessed that he came from a family where traditionally everything to do with the home and the children was left to the women. It was considered not only unnecessary but downright unmanly for a male member of the household to lift a finger to help in the house, and Michael had more than once literally been bundled out of the kitchen when his father found him there with his mother.

When they came to Step 8, 'Where Do I Want to Go?', Michael uncovered the feeling that although he couldn't understand why Tania didn't 'accept her woman's role' in the way that the women in his own family had always done, part of him genuinely wanted to be more involved with his children and with the running of the house. He also wanted a good relationship with Tania. Step 9 enabled Michael to identify the trigger thoughts that came between him and offering more help to Tania and the children as 'She's a woman, she ought to get on with it', 'It's her place, not mine', 'It isn't man's work', 'It isn't my place', 'I'll feel silly if I do things for the kids', 'It's unmanly'. Examining these trigger thoughts, Michael found they were often stopping him from doing the very things he wanted to do. He described his thoughts as 'carving out a role for myself which I see now nobody really wants or expects of me. The kids don't want it, Tania doesn't want it, and I don't want it. So why the hell should I let myself be stuck with it?'

Michael and Tania worked together on taking more control of Michael's life script by working out a contract between them which allowed Michael to take over his proper share of the household activities by stages. Tania, for her part, now felt she understood Michael much better, and agreed not to push him too far or too fast. She examined the trigger thoughts that had led to her feelings of irritation towards him and found them to be such things as 'He's just being lazy', 'He doesn't care about me or the children', 'If he loved me he'd get off his bum and come and help'. She saw now that these thoughts were inappropriate. Michael wasn't a lazy man, and he did care for her and the children.

Steps 7, 8 and 9 can lead to speedy and long-term improvements in relationships as partners come to understand themselves and each other better, and to identify together what they want from the relationship and what is currently preventing them from achieving it. Both men and women come to relationships saddled with life scripts that influence (in many cases dictate) what they expect from each other and what they are prepared to give in return. Steps 7, 8 and 9 allow them to identify the origin of these expectations, and to reappraise them in the light of a more accurate understanding of present circumstances. This is true not just of the relationships of young adults like Tania and Michael, but also of more long-standing ones. People change within a relationship over the years, and if the relationship is to continue successfully these changes must be identified and understood.

No script is ever static. Once a relationship becomes established, the partners begin to write a script together. It is useless if one partner tries to hang on to the early pages of a script when the other has long since started on a new chapter. In relationships as in individual life, we have to recognize that the life script is never complete and final; new material is always being added, whether we like it or not, and problems arise if we try to live today's script exclusively in terms of yesterday's chapters.

Identifying Inappropriate Trigger Thoughts

In relationships and in our individual lives, the wrong kind of trigger thoughts can hold up the development of much of our full potential as human beings. They can sap our confidence, come between us and the use of our abilities, and take from us much of the joy of living. We now have an important answer to the question posed in Chapter 1, 'Who is in Charge in Here?'. The answer is that very often it is our trigger thoughts that are in charge when it should be our own will or our own balanced judgement.

Inappropriate trigger thoughts can stunt the development of our emotional lives. I stressed in Chapter 3 the vital importance to our psychological development of the ability to recognize and accept our emotions, and I have re-emphasized this issue on a number of occasions since. Without a full awareness of our emotionality, and reasonable freedom within which to express it, we can never be who we really are. The life script largely determines the extent of this awareness and freedom, and it is through the trigger thoughts created by the script that it continues to assert much of its control over us.

Michael, whose relationship with his family we have just looked at, is a good example of a man whose feelings for his children were not allowed full expression due to the trigger thoughts that told him it was 'unmanly' for him to take a hand in caring for them. Many other men, because a life script which, like Michael's, gives them a one-sided picture of manhood, find they are prevented from exploring the gentler side of themselves by trigger thoughts such as 'Men don't cry', 'It's soft to say you're sorry', 'Men have to be tough', 'Winning is what counts', 'I've got to hide my feelings'. Such trigger thoughts leave them locked into a macho role which ultimately brings little joy to themselves or to others.

Women may suffer in the reverse direction, in that their scripts may leave them with the one-sided role model that women should never assert themselves, must always be there for their families, and must never give way to 'male' emotions such as anger, dominance and determination. In this case they are prevented from exploring the more positive, outgoing side of themselves by trigger thoughts such as 'Don't upset anyone', 'It's selfish to do what *I* want', 'I mustn't say what I'm really thinking', 'Women have to keep the peace', 'My opinions aren't important', and 'Whatever will other people think?' These thoughts and others like them can prevent women from owning their lives. Instead of developing some autonomy over themselves and their destinies, they remain imprisoned by their own thinking.

Women often have a particular problem in that their job as mother puts extra – and very special – demands upon them. In Chapter 4 we met Julia, who felt she was losing any sense of 'where I end and the rest of the family begin', due to pressures put on her by looking after her husband and three young children. It seemed she had to be 'who they want me to be, never who I want to be. In fact it's got so that I don't know any more who I *do* want to be. I just sort of exist somewhere in the middle . . . a sort of litter bin into which everyone else stuffs their rubbish.'

JULIA

Julia, you will remember, had given up a promising career to bring up her children, and was convinced that by the time the children were big enough for her to return to it 'I'll probably be too old and too mentally rusty to be any use . . . I'm starting to get into such a state that not only can I never relax during the day, I wake every night with feelings of sheer panic. I lie there sweating away and with my heart thumping, and feel so desperate sometimes it's as much as I can do not to run over to the window and jump out.'

Julia had no difficulty with Steps 6, 7 and 8. She knew where she was now and how she had got there ('My life script never taught me how to make choices or set priorities, or how to think realistically about a career and motherhood, because the pattern in my family was for women to be very much the doormats, and to leave all the decisions to the men'), and she knew where she wanted to go ('Out of this house every morning with a clear conscience, a light heart, and a good job to go to'). But the second task in Step 9 presented more difficulty as she felt convinced there were 'just so many trigger thoughts I don't know where to start'. But start she did, and in due course identified the three major ones that seemed to underpin all the rest. These had to do respectively with a sense of loss ('I've lost the chance of a career', 'I'm losing the best years of my life'), a sense of unfairness ('I was better at my career than my husband is at his, but because I'm a woman I'm the one who has to stay at home'), and a sense of being overwhelmed ('I just can't cope with it all', 'I never have any time to myself', 'There's no space in my life for *me*'). It was these thoughts that set off her depressions and her sense of panic.

Examining these trigger thoughts, Julia saw how closely they were linked to her earlier discovery that her life script had never taught her how to 'make choices or set priorities, or how to think realistically about a career and motherhood'. As a consequence, she tended to see the external demands made upon her as less manageable than they really were. She exaggerated their strength. They were demands right enough, but they weren't as extreme as she thought them. Her trigger thoughts were preventing her from looking objectively at them and fully developing the coping, rational side of herself. She had shown by her successful career that she was well able to handle a demanding life. Now she needed to apply her abilities to her present situation, instead of allowing her negative trigger thoughts to condition her into seeing it as consistently bigger than she was. This meant that Julia had to rewrite some of the rules by which she lived her life, and I will return to this (the fourth task in Step 9) shortly.

Trigger thoughts and self-esteem

Julia also showed the extent to which trigger thoughts can put one down. The frequent repetition of thoughts such as 'I can't cope' have the effect of stripping away one's belief in oneself. This is seen even more clearly in the case of people whose main problem is low self-esteem.

JENNIFER AND PATRICIA
Jennifer in Chapter 5 was just such a person. Jennifer was afraid of making real decisions about her life, chiefly because she had internalized the overshadowing influence of her three older brothers. Unsure of herself, she had never been able to explore the spontaneous, creative side of her nature, and felt that until she did so she would be unable fully to love herself or to love others. In Step 9, Jennifer identified her trigger thoughts as such things as 'It won't be any good if *I* do it', 'People will only laugh at me', 'I can't risk being shown up', 'I'm sure I don't really have any talent'.

Another example of the put-down provided by the trigger thoughts of people with low self-esteem is given by Patricia, who I talked about in Chapter 7. Patricia had a picture of herself as 'a little white mouse, just waiting for other people to pounce on me', and had particular problems in relating to people in authority. Patricia's trigger thoughts were along the lines of 'He/she knows much more than I do', 'He/she is enjoying making me look small', 'He/she doesn't care about my feelings', 'I'm going to look stupid again'. In her habit of mentally re-running worrying incidents again and again she used such trigger thoughts as 'If only I could think more quickly', 'I behaved like a fool', 'If only I had thought to say . . .', 'I'm never going to be able to handle that kind of situation'.

Both Jennifer and Patricia were able to see how the constant repetition of these put-down trigger thoughts not only came between them and their ability to handle situations as they arose in life, but also acted as a constant drain on their already inadequate self-esteem. Both women were also able to see the inappropriate nature of these thoughts. There was no good reason in her present life why Jennifer shouldn't start exploring her creative talents, and there was no good reason why Patricia should routinely think of other people as better than her. Again, like Julia, this involved rewriting some of the rules by which they lived and found meaning in their lives, and this they undertook as the fourth part of the task in Step 9, which we'll come to shortly. But before we look at this fourth part, there is a valuable exercise you can do to help you identify your trigger thoughts.

Identifying the inappropriate trigger thoughts that lead to emotional reactions of panic or anger or depression or whatever, is less difficult than might at first appear. The reason we're not aware of these thoughts already is simply that we haven't looked for them. There is nothing especially elusive about them. They happen for the most part at a conscious level, but have become so near to being automatic that they have a fleeting, condensed quality, like a kind of mental shorthand. At times, so habitual and instantaneous have they become – like a knee-jerk reflex

– that we register them more as a kind of instantaneous impression than as a thought.

However elusive they may at first seem, we have a big advantage in identifying them, which is that they usually occur not only when we're in the actual situation concerned but also when we *imagine it*, provided our imagination is strong enough (and it usually is) to lead to the actual arousal of the emotional reaction. See for yourself.

▶ Exercise 19: Identifying trigger thoughts

Sit quietly at a time when you're unlikely to be interrupted for a few minutes. Put yourself in the same relaxed frame of mind as in Exercise 18 by letting go of any tension you feel in your body and letting your breathing become deep and steady. Think for a moment about the particular emotional reaction in yourself you want to explore. Now recall an incident (or construct a fictitious but typical incident) that gave rise to that reaction. It may be having to stand up and speak in public, or having to assert yourself, or dealing with someone or something you find irritating, or seeing objects which you feel are offensive in some way. Whatever it is, make your imaginings as vivid as possible. Now observe the immediate thought or impression that comes into your mind the moment the incident is there in your imagination, in other words the thought or impression that intervenes in that moment between your awareness of the incident and the arousal of the emotion connected with it. Imagine a number of similar incidents. Observe each time the thought or thoughts that intervene in that crucial moment.

You may need to try this exercise on a few separate occasions before it become spontaneous and realistic enough for you to be able to identify the trigger thought or thoughts involved. But success will come. The exercise has the added advantage of making you much more alert to the trigger thought or thoughts when the situation concerned actually occurs in real life. Don't put too much effort into it, though. Exercises of this kind work much better if you approach them in an almost playful way, eager to *see* what happens rather than to try and *make* it happen.

If you have difficulty in identifying trigger thoughts, even as fleeting impressions, don't worry. Look instead for the thought or the idea that is *associated with* the emotion as – or immediately after – it arises, rather than the thought that precedes it. This thought or this idea is often an echo of the trigger thought, or closely linked to it. It will give you enough to work on.

Once the trigger thoughts are identified, recognize:

* their semi-automatic nature, almost like conditioned reflexes

* their inappropriateness to many of the actual situations in your life as you live it now

* the extent to which they therefore need to be replaced with thoughts more relevant to the life you're leading now.

Recognize also the self-defeating nature of your inappropriate trigger thoughts. Rather than serving to help you handle a situation, they are usually the very things that prevent you from doing so. It is they, rather than the actual situation itself, that defeat your attempt to cope as you would like. It is they, rather than the situation itself, that summon up the unwanted emotion. They thus often act as what psychologists call *self-fulfilling prophecies*. The thoughts tell you in effect that you will fail, or that you must become fearful or angry or depressed or whatever, and by their very presence and the emotions which they trigger they actually bring this unwanted situation about.

When working on their problems, people sometimes tell me, 'I know it's silly to behave as I do, but I can't stop myself', or 'I know the right answers in my head, but I can't get the message through to my nerves', or 'Knowing the right answer is one thing, feeling it is quite another'. The reason for these statements is that although the people concerned have dealt with the logic behind the situation, they haven't yet recognized the existence of the trigger thoughts that set off their emotions. Thus their 'knowing' is only half knowing. It's a theoretical knowing, not a practical knowing. It's not unlike learning from a manual how to drive a car, but without being told the function of the pedals.

The result is that the message these people carry in their heads never gets through to the place where it's intended. Their head is trying to tell their emotions one thing, but before it can be received and acted upon by the emotions, it's replaced by a quite different instruction delivered by the unrecognized trigger thought. Until the trigger thought is seen for what it is, such people have a very uphill struggle in front of them.

But what happens if, after identifying the trigger thought, you're driven to the conclusion that although it's causing your problems, it is in fact an accurate response to whatever it is that happens to be prompting it? You can't re-evaluate it and replace it with something more appropriate, because there's no doubt in your mind that it's telling you the truth.

For example, the thought may be 'I'm being a bad parent', followed by the emotion of guilt. On examination, it does indeed seem as if you are failing presently in your parental responsibilities. So what's to be done? The answer is to identify the *meaning* for you as a person that the trigger thought carries. If the thought tells you, very properly, that you're not at present making a very good job of being a parent, what thought does this in turn trigger off about yourself?

Usually, what we discover is that although the first trigger thought may be appropriate, the second one most certainly isn't. In the present example, the second thought is normally along the lines of 'So I'm always a bad parent'. Not true. The very fact that you've recognized your inadequacies as a parent in what you are doing now shows that you are thinking sensibly about parenthood, which is a sign that you are trying to do your job properly. Parents should frequently be looking at what they do with their children and assessing whether it's right or not. Far from the thought 'So I'm always a bad parent', the appropriate response is 'Good. I've spotted my faults as a parent and I'm honest enough to face them. Now what can I do to put things right?'

A response of this kind is accurate and constructive. And although it isn't possible to be a good parent in everything you do, there are always steps you can take in that direction, however small. And once the steps are taken and seen to be of value, they can lead on to further insights and further steps.

Let's take another example. Suppose the trigger thought is 'I missed a big chance in life'. All right, maybe I did. Now what is the second thought? Usually something like 'That means I'm a failure'. Again not so. A more appropriate one is 'So what can I learn from that for the future?' Mistakes are an inevitable and often essential part of learning, as I have pointed out before. The important thing is what they can teach us.

What if there is literally *nothing* you can learn from a mistake in direct terms, and nothing you can do to put it right? This is an unusual state of affairs, but let's accept it can happen. The ensuing thoughts should now be 'Okay, I can't put it right. So am I going to make a second, even worse mistake by allowing it go on upsetting me?' People sometimes hold on to mistakes of this kind, brooding again and again over what might have been, instead of accepting that it is the brooding rather than the original mistake that is now making them so miserable, and will go on making them miserable until they let it go.

Changing Your Personal Rules

Whatever the nature of your inappropriate trigger thoughts, the fourth task in Step 9 is as follows.

* recognize and deal with the personal rules and regulations in your life script which gave birth to the trigger thoughts in the past, and which sustain them now.

The presence of these rules and regulations was first raised in Chapter 7 where I discussed the need to look again at the concepts we have of things like 'authority', 'duty', 'conscience', 'guilt', 'belief', 'religion', 'power', 'status', 'pride', 'obey', 'love' and so on. I mentioned that we often carry these concepts in our minds in the form they were given to us by others, and that it is only when we begin to think about the meaning they have for us *personally* that we come properly to own them for ourselves.

JULIA

I also said that often we make the discovery that this personal meaning is very different from the meaning given to us by others. If we go back for a moment to Julia, with her three young children and her longing to resume her interrupted career, it's easy to see that such trigger thoughts as 'I'm losing the best years of my life', 'I was better at my career than my husband is at his, but because I'm a woman I'm the one who has to stay at home', 'I just can't cope with it all', 'I never have any time to myself', and 'There's no space in my life for *me*' were linked to a particular set of underlying concepts about life.

Julia identified these underlying concepts as having to do with *loss* ('I'm losing the best years of my life'), *fairness* ('. . . because I'm a woman I'm the one who has to stay at home'), *efficiency* ('I just can't cope'), and *myself* ('There's no space in my life for *me*').

Working on the first of these, *loss*, she identified the fact that since early childhood she had carried the concept that she must be *working* if she was to be seen as 'useful' and 'good'. Accordingly she had worked hard at school and worked hard at university and worked hard at her career, and now that she was no longer 'working' in that sense, she felt depressed and unfulfilled.

Julia identified this as a particular problem of women. 'We're pushed hard throughout our education, and made to feel motivated by academic success and a good job, and then suddenly we're expected to give all that up and be motivated by running a family.' Julia's solution was 'Okay, I have to ditch all that early motivation, and find out what I really want to do with my "best years". I wasn't taught how to do this, so I'm going to have to find my own way.'

On the subject of *fairness* Julia said, 'I'm still stuck with this childish cry of "It's not fair", as if by crying about it some adult will come along and magically put everything to rights. I have to change that concept, and realize that maybe life isn't "fair" in the way in which we understood fairness in childhood. Women who want children but can't have them probably think it's unfair I've got three when they don't even have one. My husband probably thinks it's unfair when he has to go and face a lousy Monday morning in the office while I can stay at home.'

On *efficiency* Julia insisted 'I've had this odd idea that being efficient means going out of the house well-dressed and holding down a responsible job. But "efficiency" applies equally to running a home properly *and* finding time to do the things I want to do.'

On *myself* she said, 'I've got so locked into bemoaning the idea that I don't have time to myself that I've made "myself" into a martyr, and in an odd way become attached to the idea of being a martyr, of being put upon, of having a grudge against everything, of being bitter about life instead of getting on and living it.'

Looking at her life in this way, Julia saw that she could well organize the home so that it ran more efficiently, thus finding more time for herself. 'And if I want more time to myself, I need to find something to do with that time. If I'm so keen on the publishing profession, I should keep up to date with the latest developments. And though I can't go back to being a commissioning editor at the moment, I can easily work an hour or two a day at home as a copy-editor. That will keep me in touch with publishing, and make it much easier for me to go back to it in one form or another when the children are a bit older.'

Each of us has our own set of concepts connected with our own trigger thoughts. In some cases, these prove difficult to change, simply because we've carried them for so long, and constructed so much of our view of the world around them. This points again to the great value of Step 8, 'How Did I Get Here?'. Step 8 allows us to see the origins of many of these rules and regulations, and thus to recognize them for what they are: lessons inappropriately taught at the time, or lessons which may have been appropriate then but are no longer appropriate now. Once these origins are recognized and fully understood, changing them becomes a much more feasible proposition.

In Julia's case these rules and regulations had a great deal to do with work and with motivation in life, but for other people they may be more concerned with 'needs', with 'shoulds' and 'oughts', with things or situations that are 'awful' or 'terrible', with judgements and evaluations, with experiences that are discouraging or frightening. Exercise 20 will help you to look for some of your own relevant concepts.

▶ Exercise 20: Identifying rules and regulations

Make lists of the sort of things in your life that:

* you feel you *need*

* you feel are *awful*

* you feel you *must* or *should* do on a regular basis

* lead you to *judge* and *evaluate* people, events and your own self.

The lists needn't be very long. A few sample items in each will do. Now list a few sample items of the things in your life that:

* *hurt* you

* *embarrass* you

* *scare* you

* *discourage* you

The lists show once again the extent to which you are under the control of *out there*, since they involve not just your own state of mind but events in the outside world. Our point of focus at the moment is on the way you respond to these events with trigger thoughts. Ask yourself how many of the things on the list really matter, and how many are there, like some of the things you wrote in response to Exercise 15 in Chapter 7 (page 129), simply because they are habits of thinking, written down in your life script (often by somebody else) and never properly examined by you.

ANOTHER EXERCISE IN IDENTIFYING YOUR INNER RULES

There are a number of other exercises in Step 9, Task 4 to help you identify the inner rules which you've often obeyed unthinkingly for so long that in uncovering them you even surprise yourself. Here is one such exercise, sometimes known as 'laddering'.

Start by selecting any three objects belonging to the same category. They could be three countries, three types of fruit, three sports, three book titles, three wines, three of anything you like. Now ask yourself (or get someone else to ask you) a number of questions about them in this order:

In what way does any one of them differ from the other two?

Which do you prefer, the quality possessed by the one on its own or the quality possessed by the other two?

Why do you prefer this quality?

Why is it important to you?

What makes it important?

What would your life be like without it?

And so on. The actual wording of the questions is likely to change a little depending on what quality you're talking about. But the aim of the questions is to take you closer and closer to the things through which you judge, evaluate and experience life (even if in doing so you uncover a few prejudices of which you're not very proud!)

Here is an example of how the exercise can work. The man doing it has chosen three sports – rugby, tennis and swimming – and in answer to the first question has decided that rugby is tougher than tennis or swimming, and that he prefers toughness. The questions and answers then proceed like this:

Q. Why is toughness important to me?
A. It shows I can take hard knocks.

Q. Why is being able to take hard knocks important?
A. It shows I'm a man.

Q. What would my life be like if I didn't behave as a man?
A. I'd lose my friends.

Q. So my friends only like me because I act like a man?
A. That has a lot to do with it.

Q. So I act like a man just to keep my friends?
A. I guess so.

The man concerned is brought face-to-face firstly with the fact that he equates maleness with toughness, and secondly that an important part of his behaviour is there to please his friends, not himself. The example is necessarily a very condensed one, and there are usually more questions and answers than this before one gets very deep. It is a good idea to try the exercise many times, with different objects. But this example shows how effective it can be.

Now help yourself further by changing each of the italicized words in Exercise 20 to a less compulsive one, and see what happens. Let's take each of the words in turn.

Change 'need' to 'like' or 'want'. We often assume we need something (and are therefore dependent upon it), but if we look more closely we see that it's simply a preference. We like it or want it, but we don't really *need* it. If we look closer still, we may even find *we don't really like or want it that much either*. You may for years have believed you *need* a cooked breakfast each morning or you *need* someone to lean on, but when you examine these needs you find you rather dislike a cooked breakfast, and that you enjoy life more if you stand on your own feet rather than depend too much on someone else. The 'need' for a cooked breakfast was an old habit from years ago ('Eat up, you need a cooked breakfast before you go to school'), and the 'need' for someone to lean on was something you learnt from an adult who taught you dependence before you knew better ('Let me do that for you, you'll only make a mess of it'). Certainly there are things you need, but they're probably much fewer in number than you imagine.

Change 'awful' to 'inconvenient'. Many of the things that get on top of us aren't bad in themselves. They just crop up at the wrong time or in the wrong place. Frequently we're perfectly capable of dealing with them or adapting to them provided we drop the resentment and frustration we feel towards them for disturbing our plans. The most effective plans are those flexible enough to deal with setbacks and unforeseen circumstances. No general and no business man or woman was ever consistently successful unless they had contingency plans to deal with the unwanted and the unexpected. Our contingency plans may be frames of mind rather than actual blueprints, but they're contingency plans nevertheless.

Contingency plans in the form of a frame of mind consist of an acceptance that things aren't always going to behave in a way that suits our convenience. Other people *are* going to let us down sometimes, be awkward sometimes, assert themselves sometimes. Equipment *is* going to malfunction. Trains *are* going to run late. Traffic jams *are* going to occur when we're in a hurry. Jobs *are* going to take twice as long as we expected. That's the nature of life. If we're going to live it properly we must recognize it for what it is, not for what we think, unrealistically, it 'ought' to be.

Change 'must' or 'should' to 'could'. A sense of duty is a good thing, but it can lose its value if it becomes slavish or unthinking. It's vital we retain the element of choice. Some of the values and beliefs and actions that we feel are imperative for us are simply in our scripts because – once again, like so much else – they were put there by other people before we had the ability to assess them for ourselves. It's important that we re-examine them from time to time, and come to mature decisions as to their virtue. We *could* go on believing them and doing them. The question is, are they really of worth to others and to ourselves? Maybe, maybe not. The decision has to be our own.

Change 'judge' and 'evaluate' to 'observe'. Sometimes evaluating others is unavoidable, but much of the time it simply makes life more difficult for ourselves. This is especially true of the way in which we attribute motives to others. 'I think he just wanted to annoy me', 'I'm sure she wanted to show me up', 'I think he was being deliberately obstructive'. Maybe, but again, maybe not. Exercises 2, 3 and 4 in Chapter 2 showed how subjective our interpretations of the world actually are. Far too much time and emotional energy are spent mulling over other people's behaviour, and reading meaning into what, like as not, were perfectly innocent remarks or actions. Where decisions are called for we may well have to try and assess other people's intentions, but much of the time there's nothing more important involved than our readiness to bruise our own feelings. Observing other people, noting and remembering things about them, and reserving judgement until we have more information, is a much more productive way of behaving.

The same reasoning can apply to unpleasant events. There is an old Zen story of a man living in a poor village where wealth was measured by the number of horses one possessed. As the owner of three horses, he was considered mightily well off. But one night someone forgot to close the gate to the paddock, and by morning the three horses had galloped off to freedom. The rest of the villagers rushed to commiserate with him on his ill fortune. 'Now you are a poor man like the rest of us,' they cried. 'How terrible for you!' But the man merely shrugged his shoulders and said, 'Maybe.' Next day, the three horses returned of their own accord, followed by six wild horses. The rest of the villagers at once hurried round to congratulate him. 'Now you are even richer than before, what a truly fortunate man you are!' they enthused, but the man merely shrugged his shoulders and said, 'Maybe.'

The next day, attempting to tame one of the wild horses, the man's only son was thrown heavily, breaking his leg on the hard ground. Once more the rest of the villagers hurried to the man's side. 'Now you will have to do all the work on the land yourself,' they lamented. 'What an unlucky man you are.' But the man merely shrugged his shoulders and said, 'Maybe.' The next day, the Emperor's soldiers visited the village and forced all the young men to join the army and go off to a distant war, leaving behind only the youth with the broken leg. 'You still have your son, but we may never see our children again,' wailed the villagers. 'You are indeed the most fortunate of mortals.' But the man merely shrugged his shoulders once more and said, 'Maybe.'

Many events that appear unwelcome can turn out to be blessings in disguise, while many that appear an excuse for celebration can turn out to be counterproductive. The point is that we often don't know which way things will turn. The man in the story doesn't tell us not to be emotional about the events in our lives, simply that if we persist in jumping too quickly to conclusions we are in for a lot of surprises, some good and some not so good, and that if we're at the mercy of these surprises, then *in here* remains ever more firmly under the control of *out there*.

Unhelpful as our judgements and evaluations of people and events *out there* often are, our judgements and evaluations of what is going on *in here* can be very much worse. Obviously there is a need to monitor and appraise our own behaviour from time to time, but there is a big difference between monitoring and appraising and constantly passing judgement. When I first began to practise psychology I was saddened by the number of people who used words such as 'dislike' about themselves – or worse still 'hate' or 'disgust'. It seemed to me that a life in which one was not one's own friend must hardly seem worth living.

Over the years I've grown accustomed to people who reject, despise and condemn themselves with a bitterness they wouldn't use even towards their worst enemy. But I'm still saddened by the suffering they inflict upon themselves, and by the tragic waste of time, energy and human potential which is involved. These people can't transform their self-rejection into self-acceptance overnight, but they can make a start on the process by observing aspects of their behaviour over set periods of time, without attaching judgements of any kind to these behaviours. The aim is then to look back upon these behaviours objectively and dispassionately, as if they belonged to someone else, preferably a close friend. Once they do this, they realize that if these behaviours *did* belong to someone else, they'd find much less reason for condemning them. In fact, they might find in some of them cause for approval.

This realization leads towards the development of a more objective and dispassionate attitude towards oneself, a first step towards the development of a more positive and self-approving one. You may remember that in Exercise 14 in Chapter 6 (page 123) I asked whether you had the feeling during the imaginary experiences by the seashore or in the countryside that one part of you was watching another part. This is typical of the self-judgement syndrome. One part of you looks disapprovingly at another part. I refer to this as 'I' watching 'me'. 'I' is constantly victimising 'me'. Poor 'me' wants to get on with life, to lose inhibitions, to interact with the world, to experience sensations, to express feelings, to make use of abilities, to relate to others, but 'I' sits in the background, sternly tut-tutting away, bent much of the time on using trigger thoughts and more general ideas to make 'me' feel as inadequate and as wretched as it is humanly possible to feel. Break the syndrome by teaching 'I' to extend to 'me' the same kind of understanding and support it extends to the rest of its friends, and thus to bring 'I' and 'me' closer to being the one and the same person they actually are.

Change 'hurt' to 'teach'. Changing 'judge' and 'evaluate' to 'observe' helps us avoid imagining slights where none may be intended, or jumping to conclusions on insufficient evidence. But even where slights are real enough, letting them wound us simply allows the other person to achieve their objective, which for their own reasons was probably just to inflict this wound. The best way to handle slights is to recognize their value to us. This sounds strange at first. But by recognizing that we often learn more from those who set out to be unpleasant to us than from those who set out to be pleasant, we allow ourselves to take a look at the vulnerable things about ourselves such as our vanity, our readiness to take offence, our thin skins, and our unrealistic expectations that others will always treat us as we want to be treated. And from time to time, if we're honest, the unpleasant behaviour of others can actually bring us face to face with some home truths about our own behaviour.

It's probably asking too much to say we should feel actively grateful for the slighting behaviour of others, but if we look at it dispassionately we can see that in its way it's sometimes more beneficial to our psychological growth than simply hearing the things we want to hear. It was a wise man who remarked, 'Have you noticed that all your friends like you?' Sometimes it's people who *dislike* us who give us the most help. If we're wise, we learn to recognize and accept this help – no matter how unintentionally it's given. Changing *hurt* to *teach* means that instead of concentrating on our bruises we concentrate upon the lessons life offers to teach us.

Change 'embarrass' to 'amuse'. Embarrassment is a particularly strange emotion. It causes so much suffering to people, yet what on earth, we may ask, is it *for?* The more we study it, the more it seems a highly unnatural kind of experience. It's hard to think that Mother Nature put it there at birth, along with the functional emotions such as love and fear, joy and sadness, empathy and anger. The closer we look at embarrassment, the more it becomes clear that it is largely a *learnt* way of responding. It enters into our life scripts somewhere around the fourth or fifth year of life. If you ask a child of this age what is actually causing their embarrassment, they give us a clue to its cause by almost invariably answering, 'people are laughing at me'.

Being laughed at, or, as we grow older and become better able to predict the behaviour of others, the fear that we are going to be laughed at, is the root cause of embarrassment. Being laughed at, being ridiculed, dents the self-image in a way that few other experiences can. Instead of seeing oneself as the suave, collected individual we imagine ourselves to be, the laughter of others confronts us with an apparent vignette of a shambling, incompetent buffoon. And a shambling, incompetent buffoon is most certainly *not* what we want to be.

Once we have learnt embarrassment in early childhood, and the acute self-consciousness that it provokes, we progress to being embarrassed by many things. A bad performance in public at something in which we're supposed to be expert; a social gaffe; attending a party where we know no-one; the presence (especially in adolescence – oh those adolescent years!) of members of the opposite sex; an error over someone's name, or over a time or place of arrival, or over something to do with our personal appearance. Any of these things can plunge us into the hothouse of our personal yet all too public sauna. So much so in fact that large numbers of people deliberately forgo important opportunities in life in order to avoid finding themselves there.

The clue to handling embarrassment lies in its root cause, laughter. We were taught to feel embarrassment because we were taught that it is bad for the image others have of us – and therefore for our self-image – to look 'silly' or 'different', and that to be laughed at is a reason for shame. What we should have been taught, of course, is that the accuracy and the value attached to the image others have of us is in direct proportion to the worth of the people concerned, not to the volume of their laughter. And that our self-image is in any case far too important a matter to be at the mercy of what others happen to think if we experience a passing moment of social disaster. What we should also have been taught is that to be laughed at is less a reason for shame than is the insensitivity shown by many of those who do the laughing.

And there is another lesson we should have been taught. Namely that the more obvious our embarrassment, the more we invite the ridicule or the scorn of others. On the other hand, the more we are able to laugh at ourselves, the less unkind is the laughter of others. If we can avoid taking ourselves too seriously, we can acknowledge that the things in us which may arouse amusement in others may indeed have their funny side. Most comedy is built around the contrast between pretension and performance. We set out with high pretensions (especially if we really *do* carry that rather absurd self-image of a suave and collected individual), something goes wrong, and the performance ends up a lamentable one. If we can look at ourselves from the outside, we may even feel our own ribs tickling a little.

So by changing 'embarrass' into 'amuse' we can see the joke along with everyone else, and probably win ourselves new friends in the process. We can also sometimes see a degree of false pride in ourselves – engendered by whatever false self-image we happen to hold – which is all the better for being punctured.

Change 'scare' to 'confront'. Fear is a natural and very useful emotion. When I was around eleven years old I remember reading a story about a boy of my own age who was incapable of feeling fear. He searched the world looking for something to make him frightened, and only found it when he returned home and discovered his mother near death through grief at his absence. The impact of the story on me was a profound one. I realized that until he experienced fear, the boy was not fully human. He was cut off from the real world in which, as the poet Wordsworth puts it, our growth is 'nurtured alike by wonder and by fear'.

Fear is part of the way in which we come to learn about life and about ourselves. Fear helps us make choices, helps us avoid many of the things that should be avoided, goads us into vital activity, stimulates us to make discoveries, to advance the public good, to practise necessary caution and discretion. Without fear, the human race would have perished millennia ago in the mists of prehistory. No-one should feel ashamed because they experience fear.

But there is a difference between feeling fear at the things that really threaten us and the rest of humankind, and having fears over minor things, or fears that have grown into unthinking habits, or fears of imaginary disasters or of things that may never happen. There is also a difference between on the one hand becoming the victim of our fears, and on the other confronting them. Confronting them helps us to spot in many cases their illusory nature, and in others to stimulate us to get things done, whether these things have to do with changing what happens *out there* or what happens *in here*.

By changing 'scare' to 'confront', we therefore see the things that frighten us in a different light. Instead of being threats to our security, they become part of the inevitable experience of life, designed, if you like, to help us see that life *isn't* a secure business. The answer to living life isn't to wish it were secure (since this gets us nowhere), but to see its insecurities as part of the process that helps us grow in competence, and that teaches us the skills and strategies necessary if we are to develop our human potential. To be confronted by life isn't always – any more than is the unpleasant behaviour of others which was discussed a few pages ago – a welcome experience. But if it didn't exist for us, then like the boy in my childhood story, we'd be faced with the need to go looking for it.

Change 'discourage' to 'challenge'. 'Discourage' means to take the heart out of us. To be discouraged is therefore to lose the vital energy that keeps us going, that motivates us to interact with life and assert and express our individual being. It seems obvious to say that one person's discouragement is another person's challenge, but it requires saying nevertheless. There are enormous differences between individuals in the resilience they bring to challenging events, because, as we discovered in Chapter 2, we each of us view the world in our own particular way, and are each influenced by our temperaments and the lability of our nervous systems.

Changing 'discourage' to 'challenge' is a vital step in increasing your resilience. You may feel that resilience demands enormous emotional energy, but in fact energy creates energy. Small increments in the energy with which we face events bring results which stimulate further energy and so on. The converse is equally true. The more discouraged we become the worse our results become, and the worse our results become the worse becomes our discouragement.

When I ask people in the midst of bouts of depression to list some of the things that discourage them – or in their own words 'get them down', they frequently report minor items like 'washing the dishes', 'changing into decent clothes', 'doing the garden', 'walking to the shops', 'answering letters', 'paying bills' (an activity that I have to confess depresses me a little too), 'shaving every morning', 'cleaning the car', 'cooking', 'walking the dog' and so on. For them, these minor irritations have assumed major proportions. 'They all take so much *effort!*' is the frequent complaint. I discuss depression more fully in the next chapter, but whenever we feel discouraged by specific events in our lives, and low in the energy needed to tackle them, the answer is to organize these events into a hierarchy of difficulty in our minds, and summon up the spirit to start dealing with those at the easier end of the scale. Once we've dealt successfully with these, it becomes that much easier to go on to the things a little higher up the scale, and before long we find we have the energy even to face the really daunting issues.

Changing Your Negative Messages

Changing one set of words for another allows us to begin the process of thinking differently about our lives. But it does more than that. It has an immediate impact upon the messages we give ourselves. Words are powerful things. If you constantly give yourself the negative message that you can't handle areas of your life, your confidence in your ability to handle them – and hence your actual ability to do so – suffers accordingly. If on the other hand you give yourself the message that you can handle your life, your confidence grows and so do your chances of success. When working with people struggling with psychological problems, I find they almost invariably describe their experiences of the world and of how they see themselves in negative terms. The last section above contains the kind of words they use about their experiences – 'awful', 'hurt', 'scare', 'embarrass', 'discourage'. It also contains the words – 'must' and 'should' – that they use to hem in their lives, and the words – 'judge' and 'evaluate' – which they use to register their disapproval of their own behaviour. Their life scripts have given them an attitude towards the world that sees *out there* as threatening, intimidating or overwhelming, and a vocabulary of self-definitions which centres around incompetence and failure.

Sending these negative messages to yourself is like having someone at your shoulder watching everything you do and constantly whispering deprecating comments and wounding criticisms. The lesson is being repeated to you, over and over again, that you can't manage your own being, that you are making and will continue to make a mess of things, that you compare badly with other people, and that you don't amount to much and never will amount to much.

ABOUT THE POWER OF WORDS

It is often not until people start working on themselves along the lines discussed in this book that they recognize the enormous power words have in shaping their states of mind, their emotional responses, their ideas about themselves and about the world. The life script is recorded primarily in terms of words (though pictures and images also play a part). Our thoughts take the form of words, and the greater part of our communication with the people and events that help make up our environment is through words. Hence the vital importance of examining, and where necessary changing, our use of words if we want to effect psychological change.

Words are symbols that represent reality and which thus come to colour and shape the view we take of reality. This is nowhere more true than in the words we use to think about, define, and describe ourselves. At the bluntest level, if I tell myself often enough that I'm stupid, I come very soon to think of myself as stupid, and to treat and value myself as stupid, and even to become stupid. On the other hand, if I tell myself often enough that I'm worthwhile, I come to think of myself as worthwhile and to treat and value myself as worthwhile.

Notice here the presence of the verb 'to be', the power of which I discussed in Chapter 4. Becoming more aware of how we use (and misuse) this verb is one of the quickest ways to recognize the power of language and to take steps to use it in a more positive and supportive way. The verb 'to be' is the verb that asserts our very existence: 'I am'. Yet we use it when we're talking about things that aren't me at all, but are simply descriptions of (often small and temporary) aspects of me. This serves, wrongly, to identify me with these things, indeed to define me in terms of them. For example we say 'I am forty' or 'I am tired' or 'I am depressed', or 'I am frightened/angry/anxious/slow/hopeless/a failure' or a host of other negative things. Momentarily, one or other of these words may describe my feelings or my behaviour, but none of them has much to do with who I *am*, with my true identity.

As an exercise, see for a whole day how often you use 'I am', and note what it is you are telling yourself you *are*. Then try the following day to replace 'I am' with a more accurate verb. For example 'I feel' ('I feel angry', 'I feel anxious') or 'I behaved' ('I behaved thoughtlessly'). Latin languages are more sensible than English in that they often use the verb 'to have'. 'I have forty years', 'I have fear', 'I have hunger', and also make more use of reflexive verbs ('I anger myself', 'I bore myself'. See – no magic buttons!).

Note also the power of adjectives. 'A stupid man', 'a ridiculous woman'. Adjectives tie labels on people. See the difference when we use an adverb and label the *action* instead of the person. 'He acted stupidly', 'She behaved ridiculously'. Actions are temporary things, they are what people do, not who they are. Actions can be changed next time. Labels round necks are different. They imply permanence. As another exercise, note how you use adjectives, to refer to yourself and to others. Then try to use more adverbs and more positive and supportive adjectives.

Avoiding Distorted Thinking

In becoming aware in Step 9, Task 4, of the inner rules and regulations which govern our lives, we become conscious of a number of common distortions in our thinking which influence our attitudes to ourselves and our experiences. Exercise 15 in Chapter 7 (page 129) was designed to help you identify some of these distortions. Typical examples of those that most of us fall into the habit of using from time to time are:

False conclusions. False conclusions are arrived at particularly when we are distracted in our thinking by pressing psychological problems. The two main ways in which people draw false conclusions are either by basing them on an isolated example of an event (for example the person who says 'I can't do it' simply on the basis of a single failure), or worse still, by basing them on the absence of evidence of any kind (for example the person who takes on a new job and on the basis of their performance at a previous totally unrelated job concludes in advance 'I'm bound to make a mess of it').

Overgeneralizations. These also involve arriving at conclusions, but this time on the basis of events which, however convincing in themselves, are not really representative. For example the person who finds it difficult to get on well with other people's children and then worries that he or she is going to make a poor parent.

Personalization. This is a particularly common error and involves the tendency to imagine that things which in reality have little to do with us are in some way directed at ourselves. For example the man who, in spite of ample evidence that his wife genuinely dislikes football, keeps insisting that the reason she won't accompany him to a football match is because she doesn't want to be with him.

Polarized thinking. This is the tendency to think in extremes, and to ignore the existence of middle ground. (A thing is either 'right' or it's 'wrong'. If someone doesn't support me it must be because he or she is against me.) Thinking of this nature ignores the concept of middle ground, refuses to consider the possibility of compromise, and scorns the offer of reasoned debate.

Exaggeration/magnification. This involves the habit of exaggerating the importance of minor events – for example the person who makes a minor error of judgement at work and thinks it will rule out any possibility of future promotion, or the person who imagines their partner has ceased to love them because they forget an anniversary of some kind.

Concepts arising from these distorted habits of thought are likely also to be distorted, and both to make matters worse for us in the future and to distort the responses of others. The person who concludes he is a failure on the strength of one example of failure is likely to become even more sensitive to signs of failure in himself in the future. The man who accuses his partner of not loving him because she forgets an anniversary is likely to give her a very poor picture of what he understands by love. The person who thinks always in extremes is likely to force others to do so as well when he or she disputes with them. And so on.

Avoiding Comparisons

A problem related to distorted thinking, and of great importance in the lives of many of us, is the tendency always to compare this quality with that quality, this person with that person. Certainly we obtain many of our most useful concepts through comparisons, but a danger arises where comparisons are entered into habitually and unnecessarily, especially if they involve evaluations ('This is *better* than that', 'I'm *worse* at this than you'), or when the things compared actually have no valid grounds for comparison.

Individuals low on self-esteem fall particularly into this trap. When assessing their own performance at anything, the trigger thought 'But it wasn't as good as X or Y', or even 'It wasn't as good as I did last time', surfaces, and robs the individual of the self-satisfaction that his or her performance would otherwise bring – and the realistic self-assessment that would allow accurate appraisal of one's performance actually to take place.

Such self-demoting comparisons not surprisingly stand in the way of a fuller understanding of one's own capabilities, and rob one of the chance of making progress. For example, a person who has a problem with extreme fear may come across a saying such as 'The important thing is to live one's life with courage'. He or she may like the saying, and feel momentarily inspired by it, until the trigger thought is released – 'Oh but I couldn't possibly be as courageous as Mary/Peter/Michael' (or whichever friend or friends stand out in the mind as particular examples of courage).

The correct answer to this trigger thought is, of course, 'But you aren't asked to be'. You aren't asked to be as courageous as Mary/Peter/Michael. You are simply asked to be as courageous as yourself. Your temperament, your life experience, the challenges which face you are all very different from those of Mary/Peter/Michael. These friends may rightly serve as shining examples of bravery, and fill us with the healing optimism that comes from seeing what the human spirit can do, but to proceed from this to a condemnation of our own courage is like condemning a camel because it isn't a horse. No-one is asking a camel to be a horse. And if they were, it would show how little they knew about either camels or horses.

Gaining Control

Working on your underlying concepts, distorted thinking and false comparisons in the way discussed above helps towards *predicting* the kind of trigger thoughts one is likely to have. For example, if I recognize that my concept of 'successful' is tied up with earning vast amounts of money and owning villas in three continents, then it isn't difficult to predict that if I fail to earn this kind of money my trigger thoughts in connection with success are likely to be along the lines of 'I can't be any good – look at the money I'm earning'. Similarly, in the area of distorted thinking, if I personalize issues, then when you tell me my sales figures are a little down this month it isn't difficult to predict that my trigger thoughts will be along the lines of 'He/she thinks I'm no good at my job'. And in the area of comparisons, if I see you driving a newer car than me, my trigger thoughts are likely to be along the lines of 'Everyone must be thinking how old my car looks'.

Predicting that distorted thoughts or false comparisons are likely to arise in particular circumstances, and recognizing how distorted and false our consequent trigger thoughts are going to be, help disempower these thoughts. We come to see them for what they are, irrelevant responses based upon old habits and a misreading of the present situation, and once we do so, they begin to lose their hold over us. When this happens the trigger thoughts associated with them even begin to arise less often. In consequence, if we go back to the questions we asked earlier in Chapter 1 (page 6), we find that we can now begin to answer 'yes' to the question of whether we can banish thoughts that are worrying or distressing us, we can also answer 'yes' to whether we can replace them with pleasant thoughts, and even a qualified 'yes' to the third question in the exercise since at least we can stop thinking some of our troublesome thoughts.

Once the unwanted trigger thoughts no longer arise, neither do the unwanted emotions associated with them. Thus, if we go back to the questions on emotions contained in Chapter 1 (page 10), we can now answer at least a tentative 'yes' to them too, as we are now in a much better position to terminate a negative emotion, replace it with a positive one, and prevent unwanted emotions from arising.

Working simultaneously on concepts and trigger thoughts, on distorted thoughts and false comparisons, takes us through Step 9, and in the next chapter I'll discuss how this works in connection with some general problems.

SUMMARY

As Step 9 involves four separate tasks, it will be helpful to summarize them again at the end of the chapter.

Task 1
Recognize and be more in touch with your feelings and your state of mind.

Accept that although they happen to you, these feelings and states of mind are temporary and are not who you really are.

Accept that as negative feelings and negative states of mind arise largely in response to a life script heavily influenced by others, you can take over the writing of the life script so that these negative feelings and states of mind trouble you less, and arise less often.

Task 2
Recognize the thought (or thoughts), put there by your life script, that arises in response to external events.

Accept that where this thought (or thoughts) is the product of an outdated life script it is a maladaptive way of responding to present reality.

Task 3
Having identified this trigger thought (or thoughts), deal with it and rob it of its power.

Task 4
Recognize and deal with the personal rules and regulations in your life script which gave birth to this trigger thought (or thoughts) in the past and which sustain it now.

9

COPING WITH SPECIFIC PROBLEMS

We saw in the last chapter a number of examples of what Step 9 means for individual people. It's useful now to look at what it means in relation to some of the general categories into which psychological problems are usually grouped. These categories should not be interpreted rigidly. Each of us is a unique individual, and placing us in categories is a little artificial and can even be unhelpful if it gives us the idea that we have 'got' the psychological problem suggested by the category in the same way that we may have 'got' a physical illness. A psychological problem, as I have tried to show throughout the book, is simply the way we respond, in this moment and with this particular life script, to this particular set of circumstances. Because we respond in this way now, it doesn't mean we have to respond similarly next time. Step 9, in particular, makes this clear.

We should therefore beware of 'owning' any of these psychological categories in the sense that we allow them to become what I referred to in Chapter 8 as *self-fulfilling prophecies*. 'I'm an obsessional, so I can't help acting obsessionally', 'You must expect me to be depressed, because I'm a depressive', 'I'm worried about this (or that or the other) because I'm an anxious person', and so on. The categories in no sense represent the *causes* of our behaviour. They simply represent *descriptions* of that behaviour, behaviour of which we are all capable on occasions, and which we are all capable of breaking.

When I use such terms as 'anxiety', or 'obsession', or 'depression' the above points must therefore be kept closely in mind. Such terms are used merely as a convenience of language, and must never be identified with too closely by any of us.

With these reservations firmly in place, let's look at some of these terms and the categories they represent.

Anxiety

Step 7, 'How Did I Get Here?', showed that many of us may have had life experiences which put us under threats of one kind or another. Frequent and serious illness, for example, in ourselves or in those we love and on whom we depend for our security. Over-strict or vindictive parents or teachers, wildly inconsistent parents, or parents who frequently threaten us with the withdrawal of love. A home background characterized by insecurity and disruption. The break-up of the family under especially difficult circumstances. Consistent bullying by other children. Physical or sexual abuse by adults. Economic hardship. These – or any other circumstances that consistently or traumatically rob us of a stable background against which to grow and develop – have the effect of leaving us with a persistent sense of present or impending danger. Particularly so if, as we saw in Chapter 3, we have the temperament, the labile autonomic nervous system, that renders us highly susceptible to fear and anxiety.

This sense of danger means that events which are seen by other people to offer few problems are likely to suggest to us an immediate menace. Alarm bells ring to warn us of danger. Our life scripts have been written in such a way that life is presented as dangerous and frightening, putting us under constant threat. A sudden pain is a warning of some dreadful disease. A car or a plane trip brings premonitions of disaster. A ring on the phone suggests bad news. A glance by our partner at a member of the opposite sex forebodes the break-up of the relationship. A single cloud on the horizon heralds the end of summer. The bottle is always half-empty, never half-full. In just such a way does anxiety become part of us.

One way of describing this is to say that our life script has left us with an overactive alarm system. This leads to more than just a pessimistic view of life. Events that in reality carry little threat, and imaginary disasters that are unlikely to happen activate this system, and the ensuing anxiety brings insecurity and uncertainty about how we should behave, about what we should do for the best, and about the future and what it may or may not hold. This can lead in turn to indecisiveness, to frequent changes of mind, and to a general sense that we are never properly in harmony with life, far less in control of it.

In Step 9, people prone to troublesome levels of anxiety report identifying such trigger thoughts as 'It's bound to go wrong', 'It means I'm going to die', 'It's going to crash', 'Oh god, something terrible has happened', 'He/she wants to get rid of me', 'What *am* I going to do?', 'I'm terrified at what might happen'. When examining the rules and regulations in the fourth part of Step 9, they come up with concepts that suggest that the world seems to them to obey exclusively 'sod's law', in other words, if a thing can go wrong it will go wrong, if something bad can happen it will happen. For these people, the recognition of the principle of sod's law, far from producing the ironic amusement or sensible planning seen in the less anxious, can lead either to paralysed inactivity or to an absurd overpreoccupation with even the most unlikely of contingencies.

It is through disempowering these inner rules and regulations and the trigger thoughts associated with them – by seeing them as inappropriate responses to the present realities of life – that anxiety of this kind can be overcome; by refusing to identify with the trigger thoughts, by learning to smile at them as leftovers from a troubled past, by replacing them with more positive and realistic thoughts; and by looking objectively at the world and recognizing the inaccuracy of sod's law. If sod's law were true, humankind would never have survived as long as it has. The fact of the matter is that, on an overwhelming number of occasions, things *don't* go wrong; on an overwhelming number of occasions, if something bad can happen it *doesn't* happen.

By disempowering trigger thoughts and the erroneous view of the universe associated with them, we effectively empower ourselves. If you experience high levels of anxiety, there's a good chance you also have low self-esteem. You may see yourself perhaps as a victim of life rather than as a beneficiary. Your life script may have left you with the notion that past bad experiences represent an accurate picture of what the world is really like. As you free yourself from this notion, so you will be freer to explore and use aspects of yourself that have lain hidden under the blanket of your anxieties.

Panic Attacks

In the grip of a panic attack we feel a terrified victim of events, our hearts pounding and our body sweating and our breath coming in choking gasps. Realistically there is usually nothing to panic about, we simply find ourselves in the middle of a crowd, or confined in a lift, or in some other situation that we dislike, and the panic attack sweeps over us. Panic is really an acute form of anxiety. Trigger thoughts associated with it therefore are similar to those associated with anxiety, but usually include in addition a desperate sense of urgency: 'I'm trapped!', 'I'll *never* be happy again', 'This is my death warrant', 'Oh God, this is *it*'. As in anxiety, the person given to panic has a view of the world that suggests catastrophe is always round the next corner. And as with anxiety, Step 9 involves changing this view for a more realistic one.

The point about your world-view if you're prone to panic – and another reason why Step 7, 'How Did I Get Here?', is so important to you – is that its foundations were probably laid years ago, when you were too young to have a true sense of proportion. You generalized a picture of the world from the very limited, imperfectly understood evidence available to you at the time. If the limited world of your early years seemed to contain deep-seated threats to your security, you naturally assumed that the outside world was like that too. So influential are the lessons of our childhood that this assumption has remained with you, in spite of later evidence of its inaccuracy, at an unconscious if not a conscious level. Correcting it involves working through the steps I've outlined in this book, and disempowering the trigger thoughts that sustain it. Unrealistic trigger thoughts such as 'I'll *never* be happy again', 'This is my death warrant', 'Oh God, this is *it*', are then replaced by 'This unhappiness is only temporary', 'Keep a sense of balance', 'It's okay, I can handle it'.

Panic attacks are frequently made worse because, in tune with the mistaken world-view that 'if something bad can happen it will happen', the physical symptoms which accompany them set off trigger thoughts of their own. The feeling of breathlessness and the fiercely pounding heart that often accompany panic attacks produce the trigger thoughts 'I'm going to choke', or 'I'm going to have a heart attack', and often there are further trigger thoughts such as 'I'm going to faint', or 'Everyone is looking at me', or 'I'm losing control', or 'I'm going blind', or 'I'm going to wet myself (or worse)'. Such trigger thoughts further intensify the physical symptoms, which set off further trigger thoughts, which further intensify the physical symptoms, and so it goes on.

The answer (remember Exercise 18 in Chapter 8 – page 149) is *not to identify with these physical symptoms*. They are purely temporary, and very rarely lead to the feared results. The more objective you are about them, the quicker they will pass. The trigger thoughts associated with them are simply further indicators of the mistaken idea that if something bad can happen, then it invariably will – 'I'm feeling breathless, people are breathless when they choke, therefore I'm going to choke'. Such false logic is understandable in a child, but there's no need for an adult to go on believing in it. Replacing it with 'It's only that breathless feeling; it will soon pass' puts an *accurate* appraisal of the situation in place of an *inaccurate* one.

Obsessive and Compulsive Thoughts

Obsessional thoughts are those thoughts which, although we may recognize their irrationality, refuse to go away, while compulsive thoughts are those which urge us to perform certain irrational or unwanted actions. For example, we may have obsessive thoughts that we are going blind, even though there's nothing at all wrong with our eyes, or compulsive thoughts that we must be constantly washing our hands, even when they're not dirty. Obsessive thoughts and compulsive thoughts are part and parcel of the same kind of anxiety, with the one often leading to the other. As with other forms of anxiety, obsessive and compulsive thoughts are related to a sense of danger, but here the danger is usually associated with certain highly specific threats, no matter how imaginary or unlikely; or associated with certain specific acts which should have been done but which were not done, or which should not have been done but which were.

Again, such thoughts are associated with a faulty world-view. For example, we may be victim of a life script which contains dire warnings about 'dirt' and 'germs' and 'sin' (warnings often accompanied in the past by actual punishments and by ensuing guilt), and can thus only feel 'safe' if elaborate precautions are taken against such things even when there is a highly unlikely chance of being contaminated or infected by them. In the case of some individuals, the life script even carries messages that they are only 'acceptable', only 'good', only 'worthy of love', only able to atone for some 'sin', if they scrub and polish themselves and everything associated with them, and are free from the faintest hint of dirt. For such people, 'dirt' has often come to symbolize all that is unpleasant, nasty, wicked, and evil in the world, while 'germs' have come to represent the power of these dark forces to invade and destroy us from within.

Trigger thoughts associated with the upsurge of obsessional feelings in relation to cleanliness are often of the order, 'It will make me dirty (and therefore repulsive)', 'I'll catch a terrible disease', 'I shall never be able to get clean', 'I'll be as disgusting as it (they) are'. Where obsessive thoughts lead to compulsive ones, the trigger thoughts are typically along the lines of 'I shan't know a moment's peace until I've done it', 'It's the only way to stop the thoughts', 'If I can only do that, everything will be okay'. Where the compulsion is towards some embarrassing or frightening (and almost always resisted) act, the thought is often 'Something will make me do it', 'I can't stop myself', 'It will show people what a bad person I really am'.

After evaluating the trigger thoughts concerned (Exercise 19, page 166) and recognizing their inappropriateness, these thoughts can be replaced by realistic appraisals such as 'Dirt easily washes off', 'The chances of catching anything are nil', 'Little things like that don't make any difference to life'.

Part of our mistaken world-view if we have obsessive and/or compulsive thoughts is usually that we are worthless as people, and that our lives have to be a constant atonement for being who we are. In Step 9, these misplaced 'rules and regulations' must be faced, along with the distorted thinking that supposes actions like scrubbing the hands or touching everything twice will make one happy or put the world to rights. Such distorted thinking shows that we are still under the dictates of the outdated life script, in this case a hangover from the 'magical' thinking of childhood, where the heroes and heroines of fairy stories use magical spells to transform mice into coach-horses, or wake sleeping beauties with a kiss. It bears (alas, in some ways!) no relation to the real workings of the world.

Where obsessions are more internal, like the constant resurfacing of condemning thoughts in connection with the memory of some act or other, the trigger thoughts that accompany the memory and that spark off the bad feelings are often along the lines of 'I'll never be forgiven', 'How could I possibly have done/said/thought such a thing?', 'I must be a terrible person', 'If only I could put back the clock!'. Here the internal rules and regulations often insist that you are the only bad person in the world, that nobody else is capable of such awful things, that no-one will love you if they know what you are really like, that for you there is no atonement in this or in any other possible world, and so on.

Other kinds of internal obsessions arise in response to the trigger thought 'What is the worst possible thing that could happen?'. The answer is usually your own death or disease or sudden blindness, or the death or disease of a loved one.

Your mind then immediately sets to work considering all the possibilities that could bring such a dreaded occurrence about. And the more imaginative you are, the more these possibilities multiply, until even the thought of stirring out of the house or of letting a loved one out of your sight can seem dangerous.

Where the obsessional thought leads to a compulsive urge to do something shocking or dreadful, the trigger thought is usually 'What is the worst possible thing that I could do?', followed by the answer 'Kill someone', or 'Run into the street naked', or 'Steal from a shop', and the fear is that this is what you are forced to do. The point about all these thoughts is that they are totally unrealistic. You're not really going to do any of the things concerned. You are simply caught up in a fear of your own imagined 'badness' – put there usually by a life script which punished such 'badness' with excessive feelings of guilt and worthlessness – and terrified and haunted by the fear that you will give way to it.

A similar process is at work if you have an urge endlessly to check things. As the car pulls away headed for a holiday in the sun the thoughts 'Have I locked the back door?', 'Did I check the windows are closed?', 'Did I turn off the gas?' and so on arise. Here the trigger is usually 'What is the one thing at this moment that could spoil my happiness?'. And off goes the mind, throwing up one possibility after another. No matter how sure you are that all the necessary checks were carried out before leaving the house, the possibilities for error still besiege your mind, until in the end you come genuinely to doubt whether the checks were *really* done after all, and feel the powerful need to go back and check them all over again.

The same kind of process can be at work when you have a success of some kind. Just as you are starting to enjoy the feeling, a thought arises 'Yes but it wasn't a *complete* success', or 'If only I had thought to do this, that or the other as well', or 'But maybe people were just being kind to me, or maybe I misled them in some way' and so on. There is always something to mar the success, something to come between you and the full enjoyment of it, no matter how well merited that enjoyment actually is. What is happening here is that deep down you don't believe you deserve happiness or success, perhaps because of a life script in which you were over-criticized, or in which other people were always bringing you down to earth when you felt happy or successful or in which you saw the significant role models in your life forever denying themselves happiness or the fruits of their success, and took over this behaviour from them.

When taking Step 9, you must identify all the trigger thoughts and internal rules and regulations associated with obsessive and compulsive thoughts and see them for the falsehoods they are. People with obsessive and/or compulsive thoughts often have no more (and sometimes significantly less) to regret or be ashamed of in their lives than the rest of us, and often significantly more reasons for deserving happiness and success. Their suffering comes not from their past or present actions, but from the misinterpretations with which, up to now, these actions have been surrounded.

Phobias

Most of us have phobias of one kind or another. Like obsessions, such phobias are usually highly specific, and involve a fear of heights, or of illness, or doctors, or dogs, or open spaces, or enclosed spaces, or public speaking, or birds, or the dark, or snakes, or of a host of other less obvious and often intensely personal things. A fear becomes a phobia when it is so powerful as to be disabling, and when it carries with it an element of irrationality. Except for the phobia or phobias concerned, those of us who have these irrational fears may suffer no greater general anxiety than anyone else.

Evidence from people who work through tasks like Step 7 (Chapter 6) shows that most phobias can be traced to the common fears held by the majority of us when young but which, in their case, have for some reason (an insecurity of some kind) not been outgrown. Many phobias are thus termed *fixation* phobias by psychologists. As far as the phobia is concerned, our life script has fixated us (left us stranded) at an earlier stage of development, where the disabling fear of doctors or dentists or of the dark or of heights or of large bearded men with booming voices had its origin.

But there are other phobias, termed by psychologists *traumatic* phobias, which are linked to single, very frightening incidents in life, incidents which often took place before we were old enough to understand them fully: a traumatic phobia of fire after being involved in a burning building for example, or a traumatic phobia of dogs after a single vicious attack, or a traumatic fear of the water after a near drowning. But whether the phobia is of the fixation or the traumatic kind, it has again left a mistaken rule, namely that *all* fire or *all* water or *all* dogs or *all* heights or *all* bearded men with booming voices spell terrifying threats.

In many cases, the distorted thoughts in Step 9 revealed by those of us with phobias have to do with a fear of losing control. The doctor or the dentist is going to take control of our body and inflict pain which we are helpless to prevent. The dog is going to seize us by the throat. The plane is going to take us above the clouds where there is no escape from the possibility of a crash. The dark hides ghosts, ghouls and evil men and women against whom we are powerless.

It is important that this distorted thinking, and the trigger thoughts associated with it, are identified in Step 9 and put into proper perspective. There are many things over which we have no control yet about which very few of us are phobic. Monday mornings for example. The need to avoid starvation, and to find warmth and shelter. The weather. And paradoxically, if one looks at the source of many phobias, we see not only that they carry little real menace, they may be highly susceptible to our control if we take the necessary steps, or highly susceptible to rational re-analysis. We can discuss our treatment with our doctor or dentist, and have a say in what is done to us. We can buy a device that warns off dogs. We can study the statistics of plane crashes and reassure ourselves that flying is many times safer than travelling by car or on foot.

The misleading inner rules, distorted thinking and trigger thoughts can thus be countermanded by realistic life experiences which demonstrate to us that there never are ghosts in the dark corner when we go and look, that the pain inflicted by the dentist is minimal and eminently preferable to raging toothache, and that we have nothing to fear from heights, from enclosed spaces, from open spaces, from water, from fire, provided we take the sensible precautions that are good enough for everyone else.

Paranoia

Paranoia is that nagging feeling that everyone else is ganging up on us in some way. Most of us have the feeling from time to time. But it becomes a problem when there are no good reasons for it, and when even strong evidence to this effect fails to convince us. The internal rule revealed during Step 9 by those who find paranoia a problem is usually along the lines 'I *must* be right/blameless/justified if I am to be worth anything', 'People should be on *my* side if I'm to think well of myself'. Thus personal shortcomings are seen as due to the unfairness of other people, to a conspiracy amongst them, to their jealousy, to their scheming natures and so on. Some psychologists take the view that those troubled by paranoia are not – unlike people experiencing the other forms of anxiety discussed in this chapter – low in self-esteem. Certainly they may not appear to be, with their insistence on the fact that they're always the innocent victims of other people's faults. But if we dig deeply enough, this insistence is seen to be bound up with deep insecurities about their own value. They cannot accept their own mistakes, since to do so robs them of their precarious self-regard.

Brenda's mother in Chapter 6, and Christine in the same chapter, showed some signs of paranoia. The distorted thinking and the trigger thoughts of those with paranoia often have to do with 'They're getting at me again', 'It's all so bloody unfair', 'They know I'm right but they won't admit it'. Unless the individuals concerned are, like

Christine, ready to try another way of approaching life, it can often be difficult for them to recognize the absurdity of these thoughts. Without tackling Step 7, where they are helped to trace out the reasons why they have come to depend so desperately (and sometimes so tragically) upon always being right, Step 9 can be a difficult one to take.

Conversion Disorders and Amnesia

These forms of anxiety are relatively rare in extreme forms and have to do with trigger thoughts and distorted thinking which say (or imply) 'I can't face it', 'Anything is better than this', 'I must escape no matter what'. The body obeys, in conversion disorder, by shutting down a particular function (the use of arms or legs, of speech, of sight) or, in amnesia, by blotting out the memory. Fainting, assuming there is no medical reason, is a similar sort of response in that it is also the body's reaction to trigger thoughts which insist 'I can't handle this', 'I must blot out everything'.

Conversion disorders and amnesia both exist against a background of distorted thinking which says 'I can't cope, life is too much for me'. Sometimes there is also thinking which insists (as in hypochondria) 'If I'm ill people will leave me alone', 'If I'm ill I'll be excused', 'If I'm ill failure will be no disgrace'. This is not to minimize the severity of the traumas which sometimes bring on a conversion disorder or amnesia. These are often real enough, and would quite possibly floor (in our own way) most of us. But in conversion disorders or in amnesia the individual responds as he or she does because that is how their distorted thinking reads the situation.

Although, as I indicated earlier, conversion disorders and amnesia are relatively rare in extreme forms, many of us experience milder versions. Our voices become hoarse or squeaky or may seize up altogether when we're very nervous or angry. And our memories may go blank when we're in a stressful situation such as an examination or an important interview. You probably wonder why the mind and body should choose to play these tricks on us precisely at the time when we most need our voices or our memories, and the answer is that the process is a highly unselective one. Whatever we may be thinking consciously, unconsciously all we really want to do is escape from the stressful situation. But since circumstances do not allow us to do so, our autonomic nervous system responds to our anxiety by trying to blot out everything. Physical functions such as the voice and the senses are dulled, and our memory for who we are and for what we are doing weakens. (I've known good students in the throes of an examination who have been unable to read the examination paper, or who cannot remember not only anything to do with the examination but even their own names.)

In Step 9, it is important for those of us who experience these symptoms to recognize, as with the other conditions with which we're dealing, that our inner rules, distorted thinking and trigger thoughts are applying out-dated remedies to current problems. In childhood, it was often literally possible to escape from problems (bullying children, the scenes of our 'crimes') by running away, or to be let off or excused if we developed physical symptoms or if we forgot to do an unpleasant task. But in adult life it doesn't work that way. Our problems remain for the most part *our* problems, and cannot be escaped from or taken over for us by some sympathetic, all-powerful adult. So the hysterical symptom or the temporary amnesia do nothing to provide a solution to the situation with which we as grown-ups are faced. They only postpone this solution, and indeed may make it even more difficult to come by.

Depression

Depression, like the other anxiety disorders, can be mild or severe. At one end of the scale there are those attacks of low spirits to which most of us are subject from time to time, while at the other end there are incapacitating episodes which make everything seem pointless, and which rob us of physical and psychological energy. Some depressions are linked very clearly to external events (sometimes called *reactive* depressions) while others appear to come without obvious reason (*endogenous* depressions). But in all cases, depression is characterized by a particularly deep feeling of sadness and unhappiness from which it is hard to escape, no matter what other people do to try and help us.

As I indicated in Chapter 8, the thoughts which spark off depressed feelings seem always to be associated in some way with a sense of loss. Either loss of things we once had but no longer possess (a relationship, a job, youth, young children, money, a home and so on), or things for which we hoped but which have never materialized (success, a stable family life, promotion, recognition, children, a sense of fulfilment, adventure, excitement, a sense of meaning and purpose in life – the list is a long one). Even in endogenous depression, although what has actually been lost is much less obvious, there is always *something* definable there if we go deeply enough. It may be grief for the happy childhood we never had. It may be a sense that life has let us down. It may be a profound feeling that we are unloved and/or unlovable, or that we are too sinful for redemption, or that God has turned His back, or that we have wasted our life. No matter how vague, and no matter how much difficulty the sufferer may initially find in putting it into words, there is always a lost kingdom of the mind, a chasm of the soul, a void in the heart.

If you experience depression, it is vital that in Step 9 you identify what it is you have lost, and again this identification depends upon recognizing the specific thoughts concerned. You may protest that 'there *are* no thoughts; I just wake feeling like that in the morning, before I've had a chance to think about anything'. You may even insist that you went to sleep with a relatively light heart. 'I'm okay in the evenings. I feel as if I can face the world, and that everything will be all right. Then I wake up next morning and find I'm right back where I started.'

There's no doubt that depression in the majority of cases is in fact at its worst in the morning, and that the depressed feelings are there in the moment of waking, before you have apparently had time for thought. I say *apparently*, because there is more to this than meets the eye, and I shall return to the point in a moment. But first, let me re-emphasize something said in Chapter 8, namely that it's vital if you're experiencing depression not to identify with these early-morning feelings. Just observe them, in the same way you observe the weather, then get up and start the day. Although you may feel that there is no trigger thought there as you wake, it is all too ready to arrive the moment you register the bad feelings. Usually it involves such things as 'I can't face the day', or 'What's the use of getting up?', or 'I've no energy for anything'. And the longer you stay in bed, the more powerful these thoughts become, until very soon they make getting out of bed and starting the day seem like climbing Mount Everest.

The answer – it must be faced – is to get up before these trigger thoughts have time to do their worst. Just accept that a certain feeling is there, but that it has no special relevance, then get up and dress and get on with your life. If you wish, remind yourself that you do feel this way from time to time, but that the feeling won't last. Nothing does. Don't waste time labelling the feeling as 'bad', or gracing it with a grand title like 'the blues'. It's just a feeling, and the sooner you get on with the day, the sooner you're likely to forget about it and turn your mind to other things. A set routine in the morning is very helpful at this point, but don't let it become too mechanical. Mechanical routines allow you to get on with your work but leave your mind all too free to concentrate on the way you're feeling. You need instead a routine (or an activity) which demands a certain amount of thought, concentration, and a decision or two. (Many people in depression say they can't take decisions; the remedy is to start decision-making as early as possible in the morning, even if only over which clothes to wear; this helps get the process under way.)

Don't try and blot out your depressed feelings or the trigger thoughts associated with them. This rarely works, and often, paradoxically, strengthens them by drawing too much attention to them. Just observe them (I can't say this too often), like looking out of the window, then turn the attention to more important things.

MORE ON COPING WITH DEPRESSION

It's hard if you're depressed to realize that depression can be triggered by thoughts. Your natural feeling is that it is the depression that triggers the thoughts, not the other way around. True, you may accept that it was a reaction to something *out there* which first set off the depression, but after a while the depression seems to you to become self-sustaining. Even when you've dealt with – or come to terms with – the problem *out there*, the depression still remains.

This 'self-sustaining' feeling that you have about depression is partly caused by tiredness. You are worn out by the emotional drain of depression, and by the disturbed nights it often brings, and it can take a long time to recover from this weariness. Partly also it is caused by habit. The human mind gets into habits very easily, and thus quickly comes to see depression as the normal order of things.

But mostly the depression is sustained by thoughts. I have explained how trigger thoughts can work to make you wake up feeling depressed. The surest way out of these thoughts is by taking steps such as those detailed in this book. Help yourself out of them more quickly by keeping the following general principles also firmly in mind.

* Keep occupied. No matter how much of an effort this seems at first, and no matter how seemingly 'pointless' you think it, activity prevents your mind from dwelling on your depression. It thus helps break the *habit* of the repetitive, counterproductive cycle of thinking that goes with and helps sustain the depressed state.

* Don't wait for other people to tell you to 'snap out of it', and to pressurize you well-meaningly to join in with what they suggest you do. Their actions risk moving your control over your own thoughts and actions further away from you. Instead, take the initiative by deciding on an activity for yourself, saying firmly that

this is what you want to do, and asking others to help you with it.

* Seek out a cheerful environment. Besides wanting to stay in bed and make no effort of any kind, when you're particularly depressed you may want to keep the curtains drawn, and to sit in darkness in drab surroundings. You may feel this environment 'suits your mood'. But of course, your mood *is* your depression, and therefore the very thing you want to change. The open air, the beauties of nature, the warm sunshine and the sound of trees in the wind are often among the best therapies.

Remember that getting out of depression requires some effort on your part, both psychological and physical. The thought 'I can't do it/face it' is an important part of the imaginary chains that keep you in the depressed state. Replacing such triggers with 'Okay, I can do it' is an essential step in your progress.

Now to come back to the trigger thoughts behind these early morning feelings. It's true we're not aware of these as we awake, but they're nevertheless still there. They take place in what we call the *hypnopompic* state, that is, the state between sleeping and waking through which we climb each morning as we return to consciousness. We *can* train ourselves to be aware of this state, but for most people it passes unnoticed, in spite of the part it can play in influencing our waking feelings. Usually it consists of images rather than actual thoughts, but the former can be just as effective as the latter in influencing the way we feel.

I'm not suggesting that in cases of depression you should train your awareness of these hypnopompic images. But you should be aware (a much easier task) of the mental set – the succession of thoughts – going through your mind as you prepare for sleep the previous night, since these thoughts appear to influence the hypnopompic state. Rather like storing them in a memory box as you go down into the land of sleep, and picking them up again next morning as you come back into the waking world.

(If you're unconvinced that the thoughts in our heads as we fall asleep can influence our waking state the following morning, remember that many people can wake at or near the time they wish. And that many of us, if we set the alarm to wake us earlier than usual, find we rouse before the alarm has had a chance to go off).

What we usually find when in a depression is that late night thoughts return to the subject of the depression. They don't trigger off such bad feelings as they do in the morning: during the day our minds have been active, we've been with friends, had work to do, had a chance to rationalize our fears, had other things to think about; and freed from preoccupation with our depression, our spirits have had a chance to rise. So, as the thoughts going through the mind last thing at night fail to trigger off the low feelings of the morning, we think we are better. But the same thoughts, picked up again by the mind while in the hypnopompic state early next morning, and while mind and body haven't yet had time to adjust to the day, do their worst once more, and to add to them there is the feeling of being let down: 'I felt so much better last night, and now *this* again – it's all so unfair!'

If you're experiencing depression, Step 9 involves, therefore, not just identifying the trigger thoughts that arise during the day, but also paying attention to the thoughts that arise last thing at night. Instead of allowing these thoughts to dwell, no matter how optimistically, on the subject of your depression, they should be replaced by simple repetitions along the lines of 'I shall wake feeling clear and calm'. Don't over-state the case. 'I shall wake feeling *marvellous*' is rather stretching credulity, at least at first. And don't make the instruction too complicated. 'I shall awake feeling good, and with lots of enthusiasm for the day, and with no bad feelings, and with plenty of energy to tackle my work, and with . . .' only confuses the mind. One straightforward, realistic instruction, repeated over and

over again with a relaxed mind, is what is required. It is
this instruction that is then picked up by the mind as it
moves through the hypnopompic state just before waking
the following morning. And it is this instruction therefore
that influences the feelings with which you awake.

. As with all work of this kind, be patient. You may have to
use this technique several nights running before you begin
to achieve the desired effect. After all, you're rewriting
a life script which has been in place for many a year.
And again, as with all work of this kind, be prepared for
setbacks. You may get good results at first, and then find
things seem to slip back. The reason for this is that often,
as the results start to arrive, we become a little lazy, and
do not pay so much attention to the repetitions while we
are making them. But whatever the reason, just note the
setback, and resolve to keep on with the technique. You've
proved to yourself that it works, and that is what matters.

Trigger thoughts during the day sometimes focus on what
has actually been lost: 'If only he/she hadn't left me', 'If
only I still had my job'; or on what this loss seems to
say about oneself: 'My life is over if he/she doesn't love
me', 'I'm on the scrap-heap without my job'; or just on
one's feelings: 'I wish I didn't feel so wretched', 'Why do
I have to suffer like this?' Whatever form they take, the
act of identifying them, of refusing to identify *with* them,
of evaluating them ('Relationships are always breaking up;
people get over it with time'; 'It's my attitude and not
the job loss that will put me on the scrap-heap', 'I only
feel wretched because I keep telling myself I do'), and of
replacing them with more realistic thoughts, are the ways
to deal with these triggers.

Simply understanding your depression better is a help.
Instead of being seen as a state of mind and body outside
your comprehension and control, this understanding helps
you to see it as something much more straightforward.
Some people put it that 'When I feel depressed, I just tell
myself "It's only that sense of loss again; so what? We're
always losing things in life. All that matters is getting on
with living."' Others put it that they can now view their
loss in a different way, feel grateful for having had the

good experiences before the loss occurred, and see these experiences as still part of them in the sense that they have deeply influenced the person they have become.

Depression also requires that you look closely at the inner rules and distorted thinking in your life. Such thinking may involve you in believing that happiness is impossible without certain things *out there*, like a lover or a job. Or that the loss of certain things in your life casts doubt on your worth as a person. Or that because something has been *lost* nothing of value remains to be *found*. In nearly all (I would be prepared to say in *all*) cases, our old friend – or enemy – low self-esteem is also involved. 'I haven't the strength to manage on my own now my partner has gone', 'I'm a wretched/hopeless/stupid/useless human being', 'Because my parents didn't love me no-one will ever love me', 'I don't deserve any better', 'What happens to me isn't important', 'I don't count', 'The world would be better off without me', 'Whatever I try and do turns out badly', 'It's a waste of time bothering with me', 'I let everybody down', 'It's all my own fault'.

Step 7, where you looked at the origins of your low self-esteem, is invaluable in helping you re-evaluate your life. Equally valuable is the work you do in Step 8, identifying the things that you want to change – and the things that you can do as opposed to the things that you can't in your life. Together with an awareness and a rejection of the habitual trigger thoughts that reinforce your erroneous view of life and of yourself, these allow you to re-evaluate these distorted thoughts, and replace them in the life script with others that are more realistic – and more relevant to who you really are.

Anger

Anger, like fear, has a very useful role to play in life. It can help us to assert ourselves, stand up for our rights, and get things done in the face of the apathy of others. But often it can be an over-reaction in which we lose self-control, and do or say things that we regret afterwards. In such cases, the anger is, surprising as it may seem at first sight, frequently an expression of anxiety. For example, a feeling of paranoia can prompt us to anger at what we see as the machinations of other people against us. Or if we are protecting low self-esteem we may become angry in response to assaults by someone on our fragile egos. Or if we are obsessional about order or tidiness we may become very angry at people who disrupt things for us. And any form of frustration that threatens our plans or any threat to our property that prompts anxiety can also prompt anger.

In all these cases, anger is associated in one form or another with the recognition of a *threat*, real or imaginary. We see others as threatening our identity, our property, territory, security, authority, intentions, ambitions, pride, status, integrity or whatever. Temperament (see Chapter 3) plays a part, in that it renders some of us more volatile and more prone to rage than others, but in everyone anger is the urge to hit out. When faced with threat, the body gears itself up, both psychologically and physiologically, either to fight or to run away (the so-called 'fight-flight' response). Anger is associated with fight, and fear with flight. Anger is the energy that drives us to raise our voices, to become aggressive, to assert ourselves, to resist, even to become violent.

The problem is that in modern civilized life, where there are social controls upon aggression, this burst of energy usually can't be released in physical activity, and is therefore often out of place. It puts a strain upon the body because we have to control and bottle it up instead of releasing it in the way nature intended. Even when used only verbally, anger can still often be out of place, proving highly counterproductive. It may upset other people, turn them against us, make them angry and even more intransigent in their own turn, awaken their contempt, forfeit their respect, leave them with doubts about us as people and about our ability to handle life's problems.

Some of the trigger thoughts associated with anger were mentioned in Chapter 8. They include such things as 'I must get even', 'He/she is trying to take what's mine', 'How

dare he/she defy me'. There is also frequently a misreading
of other people's motives (especially in the presence of
paranoia), and a mistaken life script that says only anger
and toughness will get us what we want, or that contains
a compulsion to organize and arrange the world in just the
way in which we want it, or that carries a lack of awareness
of the legitimate needs and wishes of others.

People with problems of anger often ask how they can
develop more self-control. Self-control is certainly of value,
but by itself it's limited in what it can do. It must be
supplemented by a recognition of the thoughts that trigger
this anger, and a recognition of the mistaken inner rules
associated with distorted thinking. Such recognition allows
us to deal with the causes of our anger before it arises.
Self-control on its own is rather like trying to smother a fire;
while identifying trigger thoughts, mistaken inner rules and
distorted thinking is like throwing away the matches that
ignite it in the first place.

Other problems

Even if we don't experience any of the problems mentioned
above, we can all identify in Step 8 things about ourselves
that we want to change. Space does not allow me to attempt
to run through all these things, many of which were in any
case covered in Exercise 20 in Chapter 8, but here are some
examples. In all instances, the principles set out in this
chapter and the last one apply.

Lack of assertion. People lacking in assertion usually
identify such trigger thoughts as 'Oh dear, I'll only make
him/her angry with me', 'I shall look silly', 'I *always* end
up tongue-tied if I try and speak up for myself', 'I shall only
make things worse'. These thoughts are associated with an
early life script that has led to the mistaken inner rule that
we have no 'right' to stand up for ourselves, that we must
let others say and do what they like, without answering
back. It is this inner rule that still comes between us and
having our legitimate say. Such an inner rule must be
replaced by a more realistic one. We have our rights, just

as other people have theirs. Standing up for them is not only good for us, but for those around us as well. Allowing over-assertive people to trample over us doesn't help their own development; nor does it help the other people they trample on.

As with other psychological problems, these inappropriate trigger thoughts have to be replaced by others that tell us 'I've a right to speak up for myself', 'It's no good letting him/her walk all over me' – and by the realization that each time we speak up for ourselves, it becomes that bit easier to do so again next time the need arises.

Inability to open up. People whose problem is an inability to open up (self-disclose) about themselves, or to share their thoughts and their difficulties with others, identify trigger thoughts related to several difficult life scripts: 'No-one is interested in hearing about me' (life script: 'I'm a boring person'); 'Telling other people my real thoughts/feelings gives them power over me' (life script: 'People will manipulate me if they know how vulnerable I am'); 'If people know what I'm really like I'll lose their friendship' (life script: 'I'm not really worth befriending'); 'Showing your feelings is a sign of weakness' (life script: 'I can't accept my sensitive side').

Selfishness. People who have problems with selfishness recognize their trigger thoughts have to do with 'I must hang on to what is mine', 'Other people never give anything to *me*', 'If I give things away, I lose my identity', 'I'll regret it afterwards'. Their life scripts tell them that giving always involves *loss*, never gain, or that if someone else has less than me, that is his or her own fault, or that if everyone had worked as hard – or been as sensible or as thrifty – as me, then they wouldn't need anything from me. Such a life script does not contain the understanding that giving brings its own reward for the giver, and that men and women have grossly unequal opportunities – of birth, of potential, of experience, of teaching – on which to base their lives.

Difficulty in accepting others. People who have difficulty in accepting – perhaps even in loving – others are often caught up in a similar life script, a life script that cannot understand why others aren't like *me*, or why others won't be exactly as *I* want them to be. Such a life script does not contain the understanding that in the end each person has to find his or her own way in life; that if each of us wants everyone to be like us, this is a recipe for conflict and for disaster; and that in an important sense none of us has a right to dictate to others how they should think and feel.

Whatever the area of our lives on which we wish to work, each of the 9 steps we have taken in this book is equally relevant. Each of the steps brings us nearer to a fuller understanding of ourselves, of why we are as we are, of how we want to change, and of how we can bring that change about.

In the final chapter, I want to discuss how we can maintain this change.

10

STAYING THERE – AND MOVING ON

I started this book by asking 'Who's in charge *in here?*', and by drawing attention to our inability to control our own thoughts and our emotions: 'control' in the sense of choosing not to be manipulated by inner thoughts and emotional processes that appear almost to have minds of their own.

By working through each of the nine steps in this book we have now arrived at the point where important aspects of this 'control' are passing into your own hands. The final step, Step 10, is 'Maintain your progress and move on': maintain your new-found position as a freer, more autonomous human being, more aware of your inner life, more confident about yourself, and more able to meet the challenges and opportunities of life. You can help this process of maintenance by learning to relax physically.

I cannot overemphasize the importance of relaxation in maintaining the advances you have made in becoming what you want to be. Psychological and physical wellbeing are so closely intertwined that calmness and balance in the one intimately affect calmness and balance in the other. If the mind is tense, it sends signals to the body that tense it in turn (in readiness for fight or flight as I mentioned in Chapter 9). If the sudden burst of physical activity involved in fighting or running away never comes (if one cannot literally fight or flee), the tension remains, locked into the muscles and the nerves. The more frequently this tension arises, the longer it takes to dissipate, until in the end it becomes an almost permanent state which manifests itself as a feeling of tightness throughout the body, or as an agitation which can become almost uncontrollable. And the more tense the body is, the more it tenses the mind, setting up a vicious circle which, without practice in relaxation, can be very hard to break.

Exercise 18 in Chapter 8 (page 149), where you observe the workings of your own mind and emotions without identifying with them, is an invaluable aid to relaxation, but there are others. To be successful, they all need to involve both the body and the mind. Working on the one without the other will never bring optimum results.

You will gain two main benefits from practising the right kind of relaxation exercise. Firstly there is the benefit of the relaxation itself. But secondly there is the increased bodily and mental awareness that accompany it. You will learn to watch your mind and body during the exercise, to check for tension here, to relax a group of muscles there, to observe how a sudden tense thought produces a tension in the body, and how the mind finds it hard to relax unless the body relaxes too. After a while this 'watching' will become a part of your life at times other than during the relaxation exercise itself. This means that you will become conscious during the day of physical tensions as they start to build up, and be able consciously (and with more practice ultimately unconsciously) to let them go again. The result will be that your body is never subjected to the mounting tension that usually builds up as the day goes on, unnoticed until you reach the point of screaming.

Exercise 21 below is a good way for you to begin practising relaxation. There is nothing rigid about the details it contains. You can adapt them to suit yourself. But the basic stages — a comfortable quiet place in which to start, identification and relaxation of physical tension anywhere in the body, attention to the breathing, mental images of peace and tranquillity, and a resolve to bring the peace with you as you come out of the exercise — are of great importance. As you become more practised in the exercise, so you will be able to run through some of these stages more rapidly, but remember that relaxation is never about hurrying. It is about slowing down the hectic pace of your life, calming your busy or agitated mind and body, and rediscovering the natural state of harmony within yourself which is your birthright.

▶ **Exercise 21: Relaxation**

Find a place where you feel comfortable. It may be a deep armchair, or better still lie full length on the bed or on the floor. Take off any tight clothing, but make sure you are going to remain warm. You can't relax if you are cold. Gently close your eyes.

Now, starting with the toes and the feet, let your awareness sweep your body, looking for any knots of tension. When you find them, gently let them go. If you find this difficult with any particular knot, allow yourself first to screw it up as tight as you possibly can, and then quickly let go of it. Finish this sweeping exercise at the crown of the head, and then check once more, more rapidly this time, to see if any of the points of tension have recurred.

Next, focus on your breathing. Breathe from as low down in the abdomen as possible, allowing the muscles of the chest and stomach to stay relaxed. Don't make any special 'effort' with the breathing, but notice how it slows down as you enter more fully into your relaxed state. Help your relaxation by making each out-breath take longer than each in-breath. This has a natural calming effect. The ideal ratio is twice as long for the out-breath as for the in-breath, but don't struggle to achieve this. If it doesn't come easily, just make the out-breath that little bit longer than the in-breath. Above all, make sure you stay comfortable.

In this comfortable state, turn your attention to your thoughts. As in Exercise 18, don't try and push away any stressful thoughts that arise, but don't identify with them either. Just let them pass unimpeded in and out of your mind. Don't allow them to set off a train of associations.

Now imagine yourself lying in the open, in a place you find beautiful and peaceful, much as you did in Exercise 18. It may be the seashore, it may be the open country, it may be in warm water, it may be on a high, fluffy cloud. Use as much detail as you can, but don't struggle over it if you find visualization difficult. If you can visualize clearly, so much the better, but if you can't, concentrate just on the *sensation* of being in this calm, beautiful place. Feel the warmth of the sun on your skin. Hear the sound of the sea, or the song of the birds, or the gentle murmur of the wind in the trees. Feel yourself a part of this special place, not just a visitor there. And as you become part of it, feel yourself becoming light and free, free of all demands and pressures, nowhere to go but here, no-one to be but you . . .

Remain in this state for a few minutes, then gently, just when you're ready and without opening your eyes yet, feel yourself coming back into the room where you started, but keep secure within yourself the feeling of peace and of relaxation in both the mind and the body. Then, again just when you're ready, open your eyes and see the room around you full of the peace of the scene you've just left.

Lie still for a minute or two, then without putting any more effort into it than is absolutely necessary, stand up and continue your day.

Practise this exercise as often as you can, daily if possible, coming back to the same place each time. Eventually it will become so familiar to you that you will be able to close your eyes whenever you wish, at any time and in any place, and experience for a few necessary minutes all the peace that it has to give you.

If you wish, carry out the exercise last thing at night, when you get into bed, and drift off into sleep afterwards. But do get into the habit of using it during the day as well, when you can carry the relaxation it teaches you into your daily tasks.

AVOIDING DISCOURAGEMENT – AND FINDING A MEANING IN LIFE

Carry the nine steps we've covered in this book with you, and work with them again as and when problems arise. Refuse to be discouraged, or to think that your efforts have come to nothing when some of the old difficulties resurface, as they almost inevitably will from time to time. If you do feel yourself slipping back at all, recognize that this is merely a timely reminder of the continuing need to keep working on yourself. Our human lives are like works of art that not only require sensible maintenance, but which are never quite finished. There are always further improvements to be made, further touches of colour to add here, further refinements to the clarity of expression needed there, further work to be done on the light and shade, on the definition of this or that feature, on the texture here, the boldness and strength of touch there.

A Purpose in Life

Part of this broadening of vision, this refinement of the skill with which we live life, is to develop for yourself a sense of the meaning and purpose of existence. I say 'for yourself', since we cannot simply take this over ready-made from other people. Our early life script, with its 'oughts' and its 'shoulds' and its 'musts', often tries very hard to make us do just this. But in the end, each of us must find our own answers. This is not to say that we must of necessity end up rejecting the beliefs of our forebears; merely that we must explore and examine them for ourselves, test them against our own understanding of life, before we can properly be said to 'own' them instead of just clinging to them by habit or by fear.

As part of Step 6 in Chapter 5, 'Where Am I Now?', you drew up summaries of your professional life, your personal life and your leisure life both *out there* and *in here*. A glance back at the exercise in which you did this (page 83) will help you to think about the 'philosophy of life' (for want of a better term) by which you have been living. A look at the inner rules and regulations revealed in Step 9 is equally helpful. Step 8 in Chapter 7, 'Where Do I Want to Go?', is another help, in that during it you identified those things about yourself that you want to change, things which were maybe linked to the way you have until now been seeing and understanding the world.

The most essential feature of a satisfactory philosophy of life is the feeling that you are living *for* something. It may be for the things you can give to the people you love (partner, children, close relatives, friends); it may be because your work serves humanity, and/or is creatively fulfilling, and/or gives a deep sense of inner satisfaction. It may be because you take a joy in nature or in the moving experiences provided by the arts or by the intricacies of science. Or, in addition to all or any of these things, it may perhaps be because you have the conviction that your life is a spiritual journey in which you serve a higher purpose ordained by God or by the great teachers or saints of history. Whatever the reason, whether it be one of these things or something else, human beings require the conviction of usefulness, of purpose, of fulfilment, of meaning in their lives if they are to feel psychologically whole.

Ideally, this philosophy of life should be long-term rather than short-term. A life that gathers its sole meaning from caring for one's children seems fine until the moment comes when they leave home and start to care for themselves. A life that gathers its sole meaning from your employment seems fine until you lose your job or retire. By contrast, a life which carries a meaning valid for all your days brings with it a surer sense of fulfilment, a surer hold on psychological (and often physical) health, and a deeper perspective against which to set the many and varied experiences that life brings.

Such a philosophy of life can come from a variety of sources. It can come from religion, from your own reading, from your meetings with remarkable men and women, from the sciences or the creative arts, or from the insights which come to you in your own thinking and reflection. The important thing is that it should feel right for you, and enable you to make sense of your own life and the lives of those around you.

SOME FINAL WORDS

An essential feature in any programme of psychological change and development is the readiness to change. Change always involves a degree of courage, a willingness to face the unknown and to take a few risks. No matter how dissatisfied you may be with your psychological life, there is a temptation, as I have said earlier, to stay where you are, to stay with the identity you know rather than to move forward. The more insecure you are in yourself, the greater, often, is this temptation. You want to stop your unhappiness and become happy, certainly, but you want to be happy *as you are*, rather than face the challenge of change.

The message is of course that you cannot become happy as you are. It is because you are as you are that happiness eludes you. The way to happiness is reached through a reappraisal of where you are, why you are there, where you want to go, and how you are going to get there – through the ten steps that we have taken in this book. Once you realize this, and resolve firmly to embark on the journey, then the way ahead becomes clearer, more certain, and much less daunting.

Let's remind ourselves once more what these ten steps are; I'll list them in shortened form.

Step 1 Acknowledge the hold your thoughts and emotions have over you.

Step 2 Find out what in your life has prompted you to have the thoughts that you do.

Step 3 Don't blame yourself if you're not yet successfully in charge of your inner life.

Step 4 Recognize that the possession of psychological problems isn't a sign of weakness.

Step 5 Acknowledge that you have the power to change.

Step 6 Find out where you are now.

Step 7   Find out how you got here.

Step 8   Find out where you want to go.

Step 9   Make the changes you want.

Step 10 Maintain your progress, and move on.

But for all of us, whether the changes we want to make in our lives come quickly or take a little longer, what we really need is to accept ourselves. We are who we are, unique human beings with unique gifts and unique experiences. All the steps you have taken in this book are part of a journey towards yourself. A journey towards self-discovery and self-understanding, self-acceptance and self-esteem, a journey which is one of the most important and the most exciting (perhaps *the* most important and *the* most exciting) you can take. It is also a journey which, in helping you find yourself, helps you find others, because in coming closer to yourself, in coming closer to an understanding of the nature of your humanity, you come closer to a realization that others, too, share this common humanity, that we all possess the same thing, a human life, to make of what we can, and to share, in as much joy and openness as possible, with our fellow travellers, whoever they may be.

I wish you well on this journey, with all its downs and ups, with all its setbacks and successes, with all its tears and frustrations, with all its laughter and hope. The most important thing always to carry with you is your belief in yourself. I hope this book has enabled you to increase this belief by helping you know who you are, to recognize the influences that have written your life script for you, and to decide how you want to change. I also hope it has helped you identify more clearly what you want to be, and has set you on the road to getting there. As you continue along this road and bring about the changes that you want in your psychological life, you will find insights of your own to add to the ones we have discussed in these pages. Share them with others as the need and the opportunity arises, for they are travelling the same path as you.

RECOMMENDED FURTHER READING

A book such as this depends not only on the professional training and experience of the author, but also upon the large body of research and clinical information produced by other psychologists working in similar areas. Rather than give references in the text – much of the work is printed in psychological research journals and is thus not readily available to the public – I give below a selected list of books which the interested reader can turn to as he or she wishes.

A. T. Beck, *Cognitive Therapy and the Emotional Disorders*, Penguin, Harmondsworth 1989

A. T. Beck, *Depression: Causes and Treatment*, University of Pennsylvania Press, Philadelphia 1972

J. Bowlby, *Loss: Sadness and Depression*, Basic Books, New York 1980.

F. Bruno, *Adjustment and Personal Growth: Seven Pathways*, Wiley, New York 1977

G. Claridge, *Origins of Mental Illness*, Basil Blackwell, Oxford 1985

A. Ellis and R. A. Harper, *A New Guide to Rational Living*, Prentice Hall, Englewood Cliffs, N.J. 1975

D. Fontana, *Managing Stress*, British Psychological Society/Routledge, London 1989

D. Fontana, *Social Skills at Work*, British Psychological Society/Routledge, London 1990

D. Fontana, *Your Growing Child: From Birth to Adolescence*, London, Fontana 1990

E. Goodman, *Turning Points*, Ballantine Books, New York 1979

V. F. Guidano and G. Liotti, *Cognitive Processes and Emotional Disorders: A Structural Approach to Psychotherapy*, Guildford, New York 1983

D. Hay, *Exploring Inner Space*, Penguin, Harmondsworth 1981

K. Horney, *Neurosis and Human Growth: The Struggle Towards Self-Realization*, Norton, New York 1970

K. Horney, *Self Analysis*, Norton, New York 1968

C. Jung *Analytical Psychology: Its Theory and Practice*, Ark, London 1986

J. Kagan, *The Nature of the Child*, Basic Books, New York 1984

H. Kanfer and A. Goldstein (eds.), *Helping People Change: A Textbook of Methods*, Pergamon, New York, 1986

C. L. Kleinke, *Self Perception: The Psychology of Personal Awareness*, W. H. Freeman, San Francisco 1978

R. Laing and E. Esterson, *Sanity, Madness and the Family*, Penguin, Harmondsworth 1970

R. Nelson Jones, *Practical Counselling and Helping Skills*, Cassell, London 1988

D. Rowe, *Beyond Fear*, Fontana, London 1987

D. Winnicott, *The Child, the Family and the Outside World*, Penguin, Harmondsworth 1964

INDEX